Medical Professionals

Medical Professionals: Conflicts and Quandaries in Medical Practice offers a fresh approach to understanding the role-related conflicts and quandaries that pervade contemporary medical practice. While a focus on professional conflicts is not new in the literature, what is missing is a volume that delves into medical professionals' own experience of the conflicts and quandaries they face, often as a result of inhabiting multiple roles. The volume explores these experiences and also the ways in which conflicts and quandaries are exacerbated by broader societal forces, including changing scientific and technological paradigms, commercialization, and strengthened consumer movements, which simultaneously expand the scope of roles and responsibilities that medical professionals are expected to fulfil, and make it more difficult to do so.

Several empirical chapters analyze data from qualitative interview studies with clinicians and other stakeholders. The studies highlight the burdens on clinicians who are expected to make informed and justified judgements and decisions in the midst of competing pressures; authors describe the methods that clinicians use to address the associated tensions within specific contexts. Two conceptual chapters follow that offer innovative ways to think about the challenges facing medical professionals as they strive to make sense of the changing landscape within healthcare. The first reflects on the challenges to clinical practice of shifting and often competing definitions of disease and associated ideologies of care. The second reflects more broadly on the utility of value pluralism as a framework for conceptualizing and working through moral and professional quandaries. The book concludes with a chapter containing suggestions for how members of the medical profession might reframe their thinking about their roles, responsibilities, and decision-making in the midst of inevitable quandaries such as those presented here.

This book will be important reading for academics, researchers, educators, postgraduate students, and interested healthcare practitioners and administrators.

Kathleen Montgomery is Professor of the Graduate Division and Emerita Professor of Organizations and Management at the University of California, Riverside.

Wendy Lipworth is a bioethicist and health social scientist and Associate Professor at The University of Sydney, Faculty of Medicine and Health, Sydney Health Ethics.

Routledge Studies in Health Management
Edited by Ewan Ferlie

The healthcare sector is now of major significance, economically, scientifically, and societally. In many countries, healthcare organizations are experiencing major pressures to change and restructure, while cost-containment efforts have been accentuated by the global economic crisis. Users are demanding higher service quality, and healthcare professions are experiencing significant reorganization whilst operating under increased demands from an ageing population.

Critically analytic, politically informed, discursive and theoretically grounded, rather than narrowly technical or positivistic, the series seeks to analyze current healthcare organizations. Reflecting the intense focus of policy and academic interest, it moves beyond the day to day debate to consider the broader implications of international organizational and management research and different theoretical framings.

Analysing Health Care Organizations
A Personal Anthology
Ewan Ferlie

Managing Modern Healthcare
Knowledge, Networks and Practice
Mike Bresnen, Damian Hodgson, Simon Bailey, Paula Hyde and John Hassard

Challenging Perspectives on Organizational Change in Health Care
Louise Fitzgerald and Aoife McDermott

Healthcare Entrepreneurship
Ralf Wilden, Massimo Garbuio, Federica Angeli, and Daniele Mascia

Medical Professionals
Conflicts and Quandaries in Medical Practice
Edited by Kathleen Montgomery and Wendy Lipworth

Medical Professionals
Conflicts and Quandaries in Medical Practice

Edited by Kathleen Montgomery and Wendy Lipworth

Routledge
Taylor & Francis Group

LONDON AND NEW YORK

First published 2019 by Routledge

2 Park Square, Milton Park, Abingdon, Oxon, OX14 4RN
605 Third Avenue, New York, NY 10017

Routledge is an imprint of the Taylor & Francis Group, an informa business

First issued in paperback 2020

Library of Congress Cataloging-in-Publication Data
A catalog record for this book has been requested

ISBN: 978-1-138-55011-7 (hbk)
ISBN: 978-0-367-73357-5 (pbk)

Typeset in Sabon
by Apex CoVantage, LLC

We dedicate this volume to the medical professionals and patients whose participation in the empirical research presented herein has been invaluable.

Contents

Illustrations

Table

Figure

Foreword

I was delighted to be asked by the editors to write a foreword to this interesting and thought-provoking edition. It explores some value-related dilemmas, tensions, and conflicts in current medical practice, and does this in an original and wide-ranging manner.

So the central theme of the book is the analysis of a set of role-related conflicts and quandaries apparent within contemporary medical practice. Along with role-related conflicts, tensions between different values and ideas emerge as important. The word "quandary" is repeatedly used in the edition and is in itself an interesting term as the conditions of perplexity and value-laden tension—or even conflict—found in the health service arenas described are not easily resolved. A "quandary" is highly non-linear in shape and form, suggesting that ready or unchallengeable solutions will be hard to find. It is most unlikely, for instance, that a simple "intervention" will solve these complex and deep problems.

The edition helpfully combines a suite of empirical chapters on key aspects of the broader themes introduced earlier (using mainly qualitative and interpretive methodologies which helpfully get the voice of practitioners into the conversation) with a couple of more theoretical chapters, along with a reflective introduction and conclusion from the editors. This is an important contribution to the field, as the editors rightly argue in their introduction: "what has been missing, however, is a volume that delves into medical professionals' own experiences of, ways of thinking about, and ways of responding to the challenges that they confront as they are expected to make informed and justified decisions in the face of competing professional roles and responsibilities" (this volume, 3).

A range of key topics is explored in the chapters: the pressures on medical professionals caused by new models of service delivery such as patient-centred care, informed consent, and shared decision-making; issues of off-label prescribing and early access to new but high-cost drugs; possible conflict of interest when clinicians become involved in the pharmaceuticals sector and role conflicts when they become engaged in policy around the macroallocation—including rationing—of resources. Subgroups of clinicians may then hold two or more different roles, which may well be in tension. They may need to operate in different worlds, each with their own values and logics.

I am, furthermore, very pleased that the editors and the authors of the chapters are drawn mainly from Australia (notably Sydney Health Ethics) but also the United States. This edition helpfully creates a greater international dimension to the series, going beyond the initial monographs which were based on work from the United Kingdom.

Ewan Ferlie
General Series Editor
May 8, 2018

Part I
Overview

1 Role-Related Conflicts and Value-Laden Quandaries Confronting Today's Medical Professionals

Kathleen Montgomery and Wendy Lipworth

This book is designed to offer a fresh approach to understanding the role-related conflicts and quandaries that pervade contemporary medical practice, including problems of conflicts of interest, resource allocation, experimental medical practices, and determinations of futility. The volume also explores the ways in which these conflicts and quandaries are exacerbated by broader social forces, including changing scientific and technological paradigms, commercialization, and strengthened consumer movements, all of which simultaneously expand the scope of roles and responsibilities that medical professionals are expected to fulfil and make it more difficult to do so.

There exist many publications examining the medical profession, from the early work of Talcott Parsons (1939) and Eliot Freidson (1970a, 1970b) to more recent volumes such as *The Healthcare Professional Workforce* (Hoff, Sutcliffe, and Young 2016). Whereas Parsons and others of his generation (e.g. Carr-Saunders and Wilson 1933) defended the lofty status and power of the medical profession as functionally necessary for the good of society, Freidson introduced a new perspective that critically examined the profession's power and the strategies the profession adopts to develop and reinforce its status and legitimacy in the eyes of the state and the general public. Much of the work that has followed has explored the various conflicts confronting health professionals, primarily emanating from intra- and inter-professional jurisdictional battles (introduced in Abbott's classic *The System of Professions*, 1988) and from professional–organizational struggles to reconcile claims to professional autonomy and bureaucratic control (e.g. Starr 1982; Montgomery 1992; Scott et al. 2000; Currie et al. 2012).

Thus, a focus on professional conflicts is not new in the literature. What has been missing, however, is a volume that delves into medical professionals' own experiences of, ways of thinking about, and ways of responding to the challenges that they confront as they are expected to make informed and justified decisions in the face of competing professional roles and responsibilities. While such conflicts might be managed with relatively little cognitive dissonance, they can also generate *quandaries*—commonly understood to be *states of perplexity or uncertainty over what to do in difficult situations* where there is, by definition, no straightforward resolution. Quandaries are often *value-laden*—a feature that, in the context of value pluralism, makes them particularly intractable.

This is not to say that physicians have no guidance in the management of conflicts and quandaries. Medical education and advanced training provide physicians with a foundation of knowledge about clinical decision-making, professional associations develop and promote codes to guide normative choices, and healthcare organizations draw up policies and protocols that mandate particular kinds of physician behaviour. However, the kinds of conflicts and quandaries that today's medical professionals encounter all too often fall outside their educational backgrounds, professional codes, organizational policies, and standard operating procedures. Contributions in this volume expose some very real, but under-discussed, conflicts and quandaries, with the goal of encouraging deeper discussion among health professionals, policymakers, and consumers.

The core of the volume consists of five empirical chapters that describe the results of qualitative research undertaken by researchers based at, or affiliated with, the University of Sydney, Sydney Health Ethics (SHE—formerly, the Centre for Values, Ethics and the Law in Medicine or VELiM). The centre, founded in 1995, is the leading centre in Australia for social science and ethics research in health and medicine. The centre's work is distinguished by its interdisciplinarity and strong tradition of both national and international collaboration. The qualitative studies reported here involved interviews with individuals in Sydney and elsewhere in New South Wales. Nevertheless, the kinds of conflicts and quandaries that health professionals wrestle with have implications for health professionals in many Western societies, despite variations in healthcare systems.

The first three empirical chapters examine the conflicts and quandaries that present themselves at the micro level of patient care, while the next two focus on the macro level of policy and regulation. However, the reality is that all of these conflicts and quandaries span both micro and macro levels of concern. This is because it can be impossible to isolate challenging decisions that occur at the bedside from the broader meso and macro organizational, health system, and societal influences that both enable and constrain clinical decisions and actions.

The complexities of relationships across the micro, meso, and macro levels have been elucidated by institutional theorists (Scott 2008). A central premise of institutional theory is that the norms, beliefs, and rules espoused by actors in a particular environment play a key role in shaping behaviours of others in the environment. To depict these effects (following Leahey and Montgomery 2011), one can envision a set of actors within concentric rings, with permeable boundaries across the rings.

The innermost ring is the personal relationship between a particular doctor and a particular patient. This core relationship—the foundation of healthcare—is nested within a wider set of actors who may have a direct, indirect, or distant relationship with the doctor and patient. For example, actors in the adjacent ring are the patient's family and members of the healthcare team, who may interact with, and whose actions may directly affect, the doctor–patient relationship. That is, beliefs of family members may strongly influence a patient's decisions about treatment, and practice norms among the healthcare team may facilitate or otherwise affect the clinician's behaviour in a particular doctor–patient interaction. The next ring includes those with a more indirect, but still influential, impact upon the doctor and patient, including professional associations and professional peers, healthcare organizations, medical researchers, and academic publishers. Pressures from actors at this meso level can take the form of informal peer expectations of appropriate professional behaviour, more formal professional codes of ethics and health service policies, and broader norms and guidelines governing the generation, dissemination, and translation of biomedical research. The outermost ring includes those with the most distant connection to a particular doctor–patient relationship but whose influence nonetheless can be far-reaching. These include regulators, accrediting bodies, the courts, health-related industries, the media, and consumer advocacy groups.

The result of this complex environment, with behavioural expectations and pressures from multiple actors, is that adhering to even the most taken-for-granted principles of patient care in Western medicine today—for example, respecting patient autonomy, giving priority to patients' interests and needs, ensuring that patients have access to and receive the highest quality treatment available—can generate conflicts and, in some cases, quandaries for clinicians. Indeed, many of the respondents interviewed for the studies in this volume speak passionately about their efforts to satisfy the expectations of multiple, and often conflicting, role responsibilities; they also reflect on their frustrations and discomfort when unable to do so, along with their strategies for managing associated cognitive dissonance.

In Chapter 2, Jordens and Montgomery demonstrate the difficulties in adhering to ever-growing ethical expectations and legal requirements for respecting patient autonomy. They observe that early paternalistic models of patient care have been replaced by newer approaches that emphasize greater patient involvement through informed consent, shared-decision making, and patient education. Such innovations are often subsumed under the rubric of "patient-centred care," an appealing mantra adopted by healthcare organizations around the globe, espoused as the antidote to paternalism by giving priority to patient values, preferences, and decisions. Drawing on studies of clinicians and participants in the context of bone marrow transplantation, Jordens and Montgomery demonstrate the difficulties and frustrations for clinicians that arise when the ethical principles and ideal models of care do not readily translate into practice. One consequence is what the authors call the "paradox of autonomy," where clinicians go to great lengths to educate patients about the proposed treatment prior to obtaining a patient's consent, but patients make limited efforts to become educated about what they are consenting to. Ironically, by choosing to disregard key elements of the consent process, patients autonomously short-circuit a process that is designed to protect and increase their autonomy. A related observation from the study is the recognition of limits of shared decision-making, bounded on one side by patients' unilateral refusals to consent to potentially beneficial treatment and on other side by clinicians' unilateral refusal to offer interventions that they believe would be futile.

In Chapter 3, Ghinea and colleagues investigate the practice of "off-label" prescribing—that is, prescribing in a manner that is inconsistent with the indications approved by a medicines regulatory body. The authors begin by discussing the ambiguity surrounding the phrase and the resulting controversy about whether off-label prescribing constitutes inappropriate experimentation of an unlicensed investigational product or whether it is a legitimate extrapolation from approved uses of a medicine. They review the policies and politics involved in regulating medicines, along with the existing literature that reports that off-label prescribing appears to be a common practice, especially for certain groups of patients such as children and the elderly. The authors point out the potential quandary for clinicians, who may have good reason for prescribing off label but risk being placed in legal jeopardy for deviating from evidence-based and approved uses of certain medicines. Drawing from interviews with clinicians, the authors show how doctors balance the need for evidence about a medicine's efficacy with their own expertise and tacit knowledge about how patients respond to various treatments, in a way that allows them to defend their prescribing decisions. The authors conclude with reference to two case studies that reveal the limitations of efforts to arrive at formalized definitions of "evidence," "experimentation," and "expertise" in the context of prescribing behaviour.

Chapter 4 also is concerned with access to medicines, in this case cancer medicines. Pace and colleagues provide examples of several new cancer medicines which have therapeutic value but which have not been proven to be entirely safe and effective and/or come at huge cost. The authors explore several challenges facing clinicians as they consider therapy options for their patients. At the micro level, clinicians face the need to provide their patients with hope and compassionate care while ensuring that the medicines they prescribe are sufficiently safe and effective. This is particularly challenging when medicines are new and may not have a substantial evidence base but to which patients are nonetheless demanding access. At the macro level, clinicians have to contend with a duty to the broader community to use scarce resources responsibly while still advocating for individual patients. Pace and colleagues provide data from interviews with clinicians to illustrate their recognition of and, in some cases, discomfort with, these challenges. They conclude with some examples of ways in which clinicians avoid or manage the cognitive dissonance such quandaries generate, including a variety of possibilities for making medicine more affordable and accessible.

In Chapter 5, Lipworth and Montgomery continue the investigation of conflicts and quandaries involving pharmaceuticals. In this chapter, however, the focus shifts from patient care and resource allocation to the relationships that clinicians have with the pharmaceutical industry—in this case as collaborators with, or employees of, the industry. Many observers argue that professional–industry relationships place clinicians in a position of conflict of interest. To explore the different positions taken by key actors regarding these relationships, the authors first discuss a case study of a controversial debate about academic–industry collaboration that played out in the pages of premier academic journals. This case illustrates divergent and strongly held opinions about the appropriate role for clinicians who engage in research with pharmaceutical firms and who seek to publish review articles in academic journals. Next, the authors present interview data from clinicians who are employees of pharmaceutical companies. Using the framework of professional regulation, Lipworth and Montgomery compare the attitudes of practicing clinicians to those of health professionals employed by industry. They find that the former group tends to view regulation through an adversarial lens. In contrast, those in the latter group embrace multiple levels of regulation as facilitators of their roles and as potential ways to navigate the quandaries posed by potential conflicts of interest.

In Chapter 6, Gallagher explores the conflicts and quandaries that arise for clinicians when they serve as technical expert advisors in decisions about allocation of health resources at the population level. She describes the potential conflicts of interest and problems of dual agency that can arise for individuals in this position. Drawing on interview data from clinicians who occupy such roles, she describes their recognition of the importance of clinician input into resource allocation decisions while recognizing the difficulties of serving simultaneously as dual agents on behalf of their individual patients and on behalf of patient populations. Gallagher also reveals the potential for conflicts of interest should clinicians engage in these roles primarily for personal advancement or for promoting a particular self-serving resource allocation goal. Gallagher describes respondents' efforts and strategies to navigate the potential tensions inherent in occupying dual roles. In particular, she describes respondents' confidence that the social processes of macroallocation and priority setting are best viewed not as issues of distributive justice but as ones best resolved by attention to procedural justice.

The five empirical chapters are followed by two conceptual chapters, which bring together and extend the observations presented in the data. While both conceptual chapters draw heavily on the sociological and philosophical literature, they offer fresh and distinctive approaches to understanding professional conflicts. Chapter 7, by Jordens, reflects on the challenges faced by clinicians who find themselves in the midst of shifting and often competing definitions of disease and associated ideologies of care which are, in turn, shaped by complex power dynamics. He emphasizes the inevitable political aspects of healthcare, many of which are reflected in the preceding chapters, including decisions about treatment options and resource allocation. He argues that paradigm shifts in the theory and practice of care can function as positive signs of a medical profession responsive to criticism, while also serving as a source of conflict.

In Chapter 8, Little explores the possibilities of value pluralism as an approach to the kinds of conflicts and quandaries that members of the medical profession encounter in their work. Drawing on empirical material from the preceding chapters, he highlights the (often under-recognized) values that underpin the various conflicts and quandaries, whether they pertain to patient autonomy, conflict of interest, resource allocation, or evidence-based medicine. Little argues that these conflicts and quandaries do not readily lend themselves to satisfactory resolution agreeable to all parties, precisely because of the pluralism of values that actors bring to their understanding of the problems. Instead, Little proposes a mode of discourse informed by value pluralism, a heuristic that enables parties to engage reasonably in dialog, without resorting to absolutism and polemic. As he notes, value pluralism requires scepticism and reflection, along with restrained partisanship in argument. It does not seek end-points that are either right or wrong but suggests pragmatic solutions that may work "for the moment." In so doing, Little offers a cautious but optimistic approach to thinking about and moving forward in the midst of seemingly intractable, value-laden quandaries.

The editors conclude by drawing together the empirical studies to elucidate commonalities and variation in (1) the types of role-related conflicts that can arise in medical practice, (2) the ways physicians experience these conflicts, and (3) suggestions for managing role-related conflicts that emerge from the studies. The editors then briefly review the contributions of the two conceptual chapters, noting that each offers an innovative framework through which to understand the variety of role-related conflicts and quandaries confronting today's medical professionals.

References

Abbott, A. 1988. *The system of professions: An essay on the division of expert labor.* Chicago, IL: University of Chicago Press.

Carr-Saunders, A., and P. Wilson, 1933. *The professions.* Oxford: Clarendon Press.

Currie, G., A. Lockett, R. Finn, G. Martin, and J. Waring. 2012. Institutional work to maintain professional power: Recreating a model of medical professionalism. *Organization Studies* 33(7): 937–962.

Freidson, E. 1970a. *The profession of medicine: A study of the sociology of applied knowledge.* New York, NY: Dodd, Mead.

———. 1970b. *Professional dominance: The social structure of medical care.* New York, NY: Atherton Press.

Hoff, T., K. Sutcliffe, and G. Young, eds. 2016. *The healthcare professional workforce: Understanding human capital in a changing industry.* Oxford: Oxford University Press.

Leahey, E., and K. Montgomery. 2011. The meaning of regulation in a changing academic profession. In *The American academic profession: Changing forms and functions*, edited by J. Hermanowicz, 295–311. Baltimore, MD: Johns Hopkins University Press.

Montgomery, K. 1992. Professional dominance and the threat of corporatiztion: The impact of physicians as the administrative elite in health care. *Current Research on Occupations and Professions* 7: 221–280. Greenwich, CT: JAI Press.

Parsons, T. 1939. The professions and social structure. *Social Forces* 17(4): 457–467.

Scott, W. 2008. Approaching adulthood: The maturing of institutional theory. *Theory and Society* 37(5): 427–442.

Scott, W., M. Ruef, P. Mendel, and C. Caronna. 2000. *Institutional change and health-care organizations: From professional dominance to managed care.* Chicago, IL: University of Chicago Press.

Starr, P. 1982. *The social transformation of American medicine: The rise of the sovereign profession and the making of a vast industry.* Chicago, IL: University of Chicago Press.

.

Part II

Empirical Explorations of Conflicts and Quandaries

2 Respecting Patient Autonomy

Some Telling Challenges for Medical Professionals Who Treat Seriously Ill Patients

Christopher Jordens and Kathleen Montgomery

Background

Early Models of the Doctor–Patient Relationship

In the early twentieth century, when the medical profession and medical education were becoming more formalized (Flexner 1910), clinicians were expected to use their education, experience, and best judgement to determine what was in the best interest of their patients, and patients were expected to accept and follow their physician's advice without question. This paternalistic, doctor-knows-best approach persisted for decades in practice and in theory (Parsons 1951).

During the latter half of the twentieth century there was a strong reaction against medical paternalism. This was fuelled by moral outrage at extreme abuses of medical authority, such as the medical experiments conducted under the Nazi regime during World War II (McNeill 1993) and experiments conducted over a period of forty years on Black men in the United States (Jones 1981). It also spread to encompass the professional hegemony exercised by physicians in routine medical care. This reflected the critical, antiauthoritarian attitudes that characterized the political mood of the 1960s and 1970s and, more specifically, the tenor of academic sociology as the prevailing Functionalism of the 1950s gave way to schools of thought that were overtly critical of medical power and authority (e.g. Freidson 1970).

Opposition to paternalism also gained traction within the medical profession. It found positive expression in the discourse of medical ethics as the principle of *respect for autonomy* which forms one of the cornerstones—if not *the* cornerstone—of the dominant school of bioethics in the United States (Beauchamp and Childress 1979, 2013). It also helped to spawn new, alternative models of care, such as "patient-centred care" and more egalitarian approaches to practice such as "shared decision-making." It is to these positive innovations that we will now shift our attention.

Respecting Patient Autonomy

According to biomedical ethics, one of the most important ways the principle of respect for autonomy is enacted in medicine is through seeking informed consent for research and treatment.[1] In bioethical theory, consent is commonly explicated as a process with several distinct elements. These usually include (1) voluntariness, (2) competence, (3) disclosure, (4) understanding, (5) recommendation, (6) decision, and (7) authorization. The first two elements vouchsafe the validity of consent: it should be given voluntarily (i.e. free of coercion), and the person giving should be mentally competent. The next two elements concern information: clinicians have a duty to disclose the risks and benefits of the treatments or procedures being considered, and their effort to do so should improve a patient's understanding. As we have argued elsewhere (Jordens, Montgomery, and Forsyth 2013), the elements of voluntariness and mental competence are *protective* of autonomy, whilst disclosure and understanding are *productive* of autonomy and also of equality in that they reduce the knowledge asymmetry between doctor and patient. If these four elements of consent are vouchsafed, the patient's decision to proceed with a treatment recommendation, and his or her authorization of that plan, can be considered valid and informed (see, e.g. Beauchamp and Childress 2013; Kerridge, Lowe, and Stewart 2013).

For broad principles and ideals to become part of the fabric of clinical work, they need to undergo both theoretical articulation and practical innovation—that is, they need to be translated into organizational policies and the routines of clinical work. Although ideas are often seen to be the origin of practical innovations, both of these processes often occur in tandem, informing or redounding on each other. The theory of consent illustrates this well. It bears the hallmarks of practice in that, over time, its elements have come to be explicated in a way that resembles an orderly procedure: first a patient's competence is assessed; then the patient is given information; a judgement is formed about how much the patient understands the process and likely outcomes of the recommended treatment and of non-treatment; a decision is made by the patient[2] to undergo the treatment or not; and if they do opt for treatment, the patient then authorizes that plan, for example, by signing a form.

The contiguous contours of theory and practice are evidence of the extent to which the ethical ideal of respect for autonomy has become a practical norm in medicine. To borrow a term from social linguistics, it has become one of the *genres* of clinical work (Christie and Martin 1997). Genres can be defined as:

> staged, goal oriented social processes: staged, since accomplishing a social process usually takes more than one step; goal-oriented, since the stages tend to move progressively towards a culmination and genres feel incomplete if this culmination is not reached; social processes,

since genres are negotiated interactively among speaker/listeners or reader/writers, by way of getting on with the activities that enact their communities.

(Martin 1996, 307)

Genres create strong expectations of how actions and behaviour (both linguistic and non-linguistic) should unfold in workplaces including clinical settings, and because the concept of genre forms the core of a sociolinguistic theory of culture, we can infer that informed consent has become part of the organizational culture of contemporary medicine.

The principle of respect of autonomy has also been institutionalized in law as the legal doctrine of consent, which formalizes (for example) standards of disclosure and creates the possibility of legal sanctions for medical negligence where these standards are not met (Kerridge, Lowe, and Stewart 2013, 356–365; Beauchamp and Childress 2013, 125–127).

Providing Patient-Centred Care

The 1970s saw the emergence of new models of patient care that emphasized respect for patients' preferences and values. One notable example is *patient-centred care*. Two landmark reports have served as its theoretical foundation. The first is attributed to the Picker Institute, founded in 1986 by Henry Picker, who is considered to be the pioneer of this model. Several dimensions of patient-centredness were articulated in what is now a classic report from the Picker Institute, *Through the Patient's Eyes: Understanding and Promoting Patient-Centered Care* (Gerteis et al. 1993). These included: (1) respect for patients' values, preferences, and expressed needs; (2) information, communication, and education; and (3) involvement of family and friends. The second noteworthy articulation of patient-centred care emerged from the Institute of Medicine's 2001 report *Crossing the Quality Chasm*, which was the result of an extensive study aimed at improving the quality of healthcare in the United States. The report identified six dimensions of quality in regards to what healthcare should be: (1) safe, (2) effective, (3) timely, (4) efficient, (5) equitable, and (6) *patient-centred*. The latter was further articulated to mean "providing care that is respectful of and responsive to individual patient preferences, needs, and values and *ensuring that patient values guide all clinical decisions*" (Institute of Medicine 2001, 3, emphasis added). The report further clarified that patient-centredness should consider "*the patient [as] the source of control*" in decisions about his or her care (Institute of Medicine 2001, 304, emphasis added). This ideal has been succinctly captured in the rallying call "Nothing about me without me" (Delbanco et al. 2001).

Although there is no single practical process or innovation through which the dimensions of patient-centred care have become embedded in the routines of clinical work, this model of care involves goals and activities which overlap with those of informed consent—notably the active participation of patients in decisions about their care and patient education.

Models of care that seek to enable a more active role for patients in decisions about their care were initially criticized by professionals who argued that they pose challenges to medical judgement from a lay public who lack appropriate education and expertise (e.g. Haug 1973). Others, including the growing voice of patient advocates, came to regard it as a moral imperative to foster more involved, informed, educated, and self-aware patients. The success of this approach again lies in the practice of medicine. Patient involvement in clinical decision-making has been formalized in some areas of practice, both theoretically using decision theory (Sadegh-Zadeh 2015) and practically through the development of decision aids that are designed to elicit, quantify, and incorporate patient values (e.g. Martinez et al. 2015). Shared decision-making also occurs informally in routine communication between patients and clinical staff. The practicability of this approach is clearly uneven across different domains of practice, however. There is less scope for it in emergency medicine than in cancer care, for example. And unlike consent, it has not yet been enshrined in law.

Patient education is a practical activity that helps to enable both informed consent and patient participation in decision-making. We have commented elsewhere on the increasing importance that has come to be placed on the informational elements of consent (Jordens, Montgomery, and Forsyth 2013). The importance of patient education to patient-centred care is plainly stated in theory, and its practical importance—that is, facilitating patient's participation in shared decision-making—is clearly signalled by the kind of criticism initially levelled at this ideal (see earlier). It is, therefore, unsurprising that in the latter decades of the twentieth century the literature on patient education mushroomed, and it spawned new roles for educators within a wide variety of healthcare settings as practitioners sought to ensure that information was imparted to patients in an understandable way (Korsch 1989; Roter and Hall 2006).

In some quarters, these efforts were thought to be a valuable mechanism for improving patient compliance with medical advice (DiMatteo et al. 2002), again reflecting a doctor-knows-best mindset. However, the term "compliance" with medical advice was gradually replaced by "adherence to" or "alignment with" medical recommendations to signal that patients were not expected to obediently follow medical advice but rather had a choice about whether to "adhere" to recommendations or to behave in ways that "aligned" with them. If patient education is viewed not as a means to secure compliance so much as a means to increase patient autonomy and enable their participation in decisions about their care, we must also entertain the prospect that patient preferences and decisions may *diverge* from clinicians' advice and recommendations (Barry et al. 1995; Hibbard 2007).

With this point in mind, we shall change tack. So far, we have focused on the *confluence* of theories and practices that have supplanted medical paternalism. In the sections that follow, we shall focus on a domain of practice where there is scope for innovation—and where there has been actual innovation—that aims to improve consent processes and make care more "patient-centred" through shared decision-making. But we shall henceforth focus on several telling points of tension and *lack* of confluence between principles and ideals and actual practice, drawing on a series of empirical observations garnered in two qualitative studies conducted in a bone marrow transplantation setting.

Illustrations From the Context of High-Risk Therapy

Study Setting

Bone marrow transplantation (BMT) is a complex sequence of procedures used to treat advanced cancer and several other life-threatening conditions.[3] It is extremely challenging for patients and is usually recommended only after clinicians have determined that there are no better options or when it provides the best chance of disease-free, long-term survival. Professionals' decisions to recommend BMT, and patients' decisions to consent to it, thus typically involve complex trade-offs between probable harms and benefits.

Many of the procedures and entities involved in BMT will be new to the majority of patients (e.g. human leucocyte antigen typing and stem cells), and they encounter a raft of new technical terms. Professionals working in the BMT setting thus face a considerable challenge when it comes to educating and informing patients for the purposes of securing informed consent and enabling shared decision-making.

Participants and Methods

The first of the two studies focused on consent and involved interviews with sixteen specialist clinicians involved in the care of BMT patients in three different teaching hospitals in Sydney, Australia. This included seven transplant haematologists, three nurses, two transplant coordinators, one care coordinator, one radiation oncologist, one patient representative, and one social worker. Interviews with the transplant haematologists focused on their interactions with patients and their lay carers during consultations, and interviews with the other transplant team members focused on their role in providing patients with information about the procedure and its side effects and the patients' involvement in the consent process.

The second of the two studies focused on the experiences of patients undergoing autologous BMT. This procedure involves the administration of high doses of chemotherapy targeted to the patient's disease, followed by the reinfusion of the patient's own stem cells. The stem cells have no anti-cancer properties or adverse effects; they "rescue" the patient from doses of chemotherapy that would otherwise destroy the patient's bone marrow and, thereby, their body's ability to fight infection.[4] Our study involved interviews with ten patients who were newly admitted to a large teaching hospital in Sydney to undergo this procedure. We also conducted interviews with a lay carer (e.g. a spouse or parent or other close family member or friend) nominated by each patient. Participants were interviewed just before the treatment started, three months after completion, and every six months thereafter (up to six interviews). In all, sixty-nine interviews were completed between 2007 and 2009. The researchers also undertook some ethnographic observation, for example, by sitting in on patient education forums.

All interviews were semi-structured and were conducted by experienced researchers in a private setting and typically lasted for about an hour. They were digitally recorded and professionally transcribed. Interviews and observations were analyzed using an interpretive approach that drew on the literature of bioethics and medical sociology to make sense of content and observations. Both studies were approved by the Human Research Ethics Committee at of the University of Sydney and by the Human Research Ethics Committees responsible for each of the participating hospitals, in accordance with ethical standards of Australia's National Health and Medical Research Council.[5]

Blame Games

In the hospital where we recruited the BMT patients, the educational efforts of the transplant team were clearly evident, and they were not confined to consultations. They included printed resources (e.g. Bone Marrow Transplant Network NSW 2006) and a half-day education forum run by staff of the transplant unit. Notwithstanding these efforts, however, it was evident from the interviews that some patients still had a poor understanding of the treatment:

> At the moment my cells in my body I guess are friendly cells, and they're accepting the cancer. . . . They're not fighting it. . . . So they've frozen my stem cells, and they're gonna take every single bad cell out of me and then put my stem cells back in. . . . Hopefully it will produce proper cells, angry cells, to fight the cancer.

This statement is mistaken because it is the chemotherapy that "fights" the cancer. The stem cells "rescue" the patient from complete destruction of their bone marrow.

As will become apparent, and as we have reported elsewhere (Jordens, Montgomery, and Forsyth 2013), the clinical staff had strong expectations that patients engage with their educational efforts. It is likely that some patients were unable to meet these expectations due to practical barriers. For example, the low attendance rate at the educational forum was likely due in part to factors such as travel costs, language barriers, and urgency of admission (Ferguson, Jordens, and Gilroy 2009). Notably, however, there was a subgroup of patients who *chose* not to attend the educational forum and/or who wilfully resisted attempts to inform them by adopting a "wake-me-when-it's-over" attitude, as indicated by the following quotes from members of the transplant team:

> Some patients will say very specifically 'Don't tell me about it, I don't want to know.'

> One girl pulled the blankets up over her head when you tried to talk to her.

In our interviews with clinicians, it became evident that such patients became the target of adverse moral judgements, for example, that they were unreasonable, unrealistic, or glib:

> There are clearly patients who don't want to know anything, but I think it's unreasonable. It's an unreasonable expectation of me to take into a transplant a patient who hasn't been told at least some very basic information.

> If he [the patient] says, 'That's not going to happen to me,' that would start alarm bells ringing, because then I would say this person does not have a realistic expectation about what will happen or what could happen.

> Often they [the patients] won't ask me questions, so they let me rave on, which actually worries me a bit. . . . At the end, I say to them 'So let me just check something with you. You understand that you may die actually having this? This is pretty serious.'

This, in turn, provoked a degree of dismay:

> I mean what can you do? All you can do—I mean, we feel that we're obliged to explain some things . . . if she stops you telling her, then that's her choice.

A paradox is signalled here. Clinicians are obliged to explain things during the consent process because this fulfils the fundamental ethical principle of respect for autonomy, but some patients exercise their autonomy by choosing not to engage with clinicians' efforts to inform them. In other words, they choose to skip over the informational elements of consent (or the informational stages of the consent process) and cut straight to the decision and authorization elements/steps of consent.

Dismay turned to a different kind of uneasiness if patients complained, during the post-transplant recovery period, that they would not have agreed to the transplant had they been adequately forewarned of what was to come. This kind of complaint is likely to trigger concerns about possible legal trouble for physicians. It could, for example, form grounds for a case of negligence against the physician on the basis of "failure to disclose material risks" (Kerridge, Lowe, and Stewart 2013). This explains why such a complaint drew a defensive response that shifted the blame back onto the patients:

> [recounting a conversation with a patient] Well, you know, you were given the option to come to the patient information day, you didn't want to come—this would have all been explained for you at the patient information day.

> A man we had in here recently refused to read any information, he declined to come to the information day . . . he felt that God would cure him, and then he got here and the whole process started. That's when he started asking questions, and then he was giving the impression that he hadn't been informed.

> Sometimes afterwards patients will say, 'If I'd known it was like this, I wouldn't have done it.' I say, 'Well, we talked about it, I showed you the pictures, I said you can die from this, you can't get much sicker than that' and they say 'Yeah, but I just didn't realize it.'

Some members of the transplant team who were not physicians deflected this kind of complaint by blaming the physicians for being unapproachable or for being poor communicators:

> Depending on how approachable the doctors are and how clued in they are to the situation, you know sometimes they're helpful and sometimes they're not, quite honestly.

> They [the transplant haematologists] have never learned . . . they don't have the skill [to communicate well] . . . that's the sadness, that people can be intellectually and academically so clever, but they can't communicate with their patients. And that's just so disheartening because you can do more harm than good.

Difficult Scenarios

As well as observing the blame games described previously, we observed several difficult scenarios that arose from a divergence between patients' preferences and values and clinicians' decisions and recommendations. One of these came to light in incidental discussions with physicians about a case that was unfolding around the time we were doing our study. It involved a patient who was undergoing autologous BMT and who, after undergoing high-dose chemotherapy, refused to have any further treatment and demanded to have her stem cells back. This case illustrates a lack of understanding to the extent that the patient was demanding something that was going happen anyway. It also prompts us to consider the following thought experiment: what would happen if the patient withdrew her consent to undergo the stem cell reinfusion in full knowledge that the consequences of such a decision would be tantamount to a slow, awful suicide? In all likelihood, the transplant team would try to persuade the patient to reverse this decision. If these efforts were unsuccessful, the team would probably seek to recruit the assistance of her family, the hospital psychiatrist, and its clinical ethics consultant. If the patient still remained steadfast in her decision, the hospital might turn to a court of law. And *even if* the patient were shown to be fully competent, and under no duress, and fully cognizant of the implications of her decision, it is highly likely that the health professionals would persist in their opposition to it. It is highly *un*likely that they would defer to the patient's decision out of respect for her autonomy (or, at least, they would do so only after all avenues of opposition had been exhausted). Granted that this scenario is unlikely to occur, our point concerns the likely response of the professionals involved.

Another difficult scenario can occur before the treatment protocol has begun, where a patient refuses a treatment recommendation while having a thorough and sound understanding of the process and likely outcomes of both treatment and non-treatment. Our study did not include any patients who chose *not* to undergo BMT because we recruited patients on admission to the transplant clinic. Furthermore, refusals are rare in this setting because the treatment is usually a last-ditch effort to prevent death due to recurrent malignant disease. Nevertheless, there are reports of such cases in the literature, and they illustrate that refusals of treatment prompt a thorough investigation of a patient's decision-making capacity and the influence of others upon it (see, e.g. Stein et al. 1998; Oppenheim et al. 2002).[6] Our point here is that a patient's decision to halt or refuse a recommended treatment is not accepted at face value by medical professionals who respect the patient's preferences and values by acting in accordance with that decision. Rather, the situation is framed as an ethical quandary, and the patient's autonomy is placed under the hermeneutics of suspicion.

Another difficult situation can occur when the treatment protocol has concluded and the transplant team decides not to offer further medical treatment, against the wishes of the patient or the patient's family. Situations such as these did arise during our study, and interviews with members of the patient's family revealed feelings of abandonment, hopelessness, and dismay, as indicated by these quotes from interviews with lay carers:

> To me it felt like the doctors had given up, you know. . . . It wasn't even long after the stem cell that they said "Sorry, we can't do anything more for you." . . . When we left the hospital, we felt like the doctors had just given up on us. "Go home and die."

> The oncology announce that they can't do anything about it, she will die. . . . I thought [this] is a big hospital, is supposed to have a more, like, machine and those kind of things, you know, and do something about

it. Basically, it's like hopeless . . . they don't have anything they can do. They can't do anything to save her. . . . I told him, I looked at him, and I know there's another machine there.

Such clinical decisions exemplify what are called "futility determinations." A decision is made by medical professionals that further treatment cannot attain a physiological goal such as stopping the spread of malignant disease (physiological futility) or that further treatment is not in the patient's best interest (normative futility) (Kite and Wilkinson 2002). There is an extensive literature on this topic that we do not propose to summarize here.[7] Suffice it to say that, like refusals of treatment, futility determinations represent a divergence between patients' preferences and values and clinicians' decisions and recommendations, and they are likely to occur in settings where there are last-ditch attempts to halt the progression of a serious illness.

Discussion

Our interviews reveal a number of challenges that arise from efforts on the part of healthcare professionals working in the BMT setting to respect patient autonomy. The interviews also highlight limits within which patient education and shared decision-making is possible. We discuss these findings in order to highlight the kind of insights that qualitative research offers to those who seek to incorporate ethical principles and ideal models of care into both clinical practice and the organizations that provide clinical care.

Frustration and Its Consequences

Our interviews revealed at least three sources of frustration for physicians and other health professionals working in the BMT setting. The first arises from falling short of a goal. Notwithstanding intensive educational efforts, patient understanding is almost always incomplete, and even after intensive educational efforts, some patients fail to understand key facts, such as the basic rationale for a stem cell "transplant" (i.e. that it essentially enables the administration of highly toxic doses of chemotherapy). Furthermore, sometimes patients' understanding is more than incomplete: patients can *misconstrue* the purpose of a stem cell rescue, for example, by mistakenly attributing an allopathic power to the stem cells.

A second source of frustration, and one closely related to the first, arises from the incompleteness of a genre. Where the genre of consent is incomplete, the expectations that it creates are frustrated, such as the expectation that understanding comes *before* an irreversible decision to authorize a risky and onerous medical procedure. This expectation is perfectly rational, but rational processes like consent sometimes founder on the limits of linguistic communication. For example, one of the recent innovations in patient education—and one that has been pioneered in cancer medicine—is the practice of inviting former patients (cancer survivors) to share narratives of their own personal experience during the education process leading up to treatment. This was part of the education day at the hospital we studied, but as some of the patients' complaints reported earlier indicate (and as we have argued elsewhere), there are limits to the degree to which it is possible to forewarn patients of the extreme experience they are about to undergo (Little et al. 2008).[8] The upshot is that in BMT, patients come to understand important facts, such as the onerousness of high-dose chemotherapy, in the main retrospectively. This is frustrating for professionals who are heavily invested in rational systems. Perhaps they can take comfort in the thought that this is no different in other spheres of life. As a philosophical truism puts it, life is lived forward in time but understood backward.

A third source of frustration arises from a paradox. If the incompleteness of the consent process is considered as the effect of patients exercising their autonomy, then by choosing to disregard elements of the consent process, patients autonomously frustrate a process that is designed to protect and increase their autonomy. This paradox has no obvious solution, which is frustrating.

These frustrations give rise to some challenging consequences, which include unfair blame and strained relationships. Patients in this setting are sometimes negatively judged for failing to fulfil expectations that they may not be aware of, including expectations to engage with the educational efforts put in place for their benefit (Jordens, Montgomery, and Forsyth 2013). There is also unfairness in the adverse judgements placed on physicians as a result of the "autonomy paradox," and it arises from the *asymmetry* of those sanctions: it is one thing to be *blamed* for a patient's lack of understanding (i.e. to face negative judgements from one's co-workers) and quite another to be *sued* for failing to meet standards of disclosure (i.e. to face legal sanctions). In other words, the consequences that flow from patients autonomously opting out of the education process are potentially more serious for medical professionals than for patients.

This leads us to extend an inference that we made in our study of patients: judgemental attitudes can put relationships under strain, and in this case not only relationships between physicians and patients but also relationships between physicians and other health professionals. Furthermore, given the vulnerability of physicians to legal action for not meeting standards of disclosure, relationships with patients can also be strained by perceiving them as potential litigants.

Two Final Points About Autonomy

Our empirical investigations lead us to two concluding points about respect for patient autonomy. One is that, in most clinical situations, patient autonomy (like the element of understanding) is neither completely present nor completely absent. It endures to the extent that it can be exercised under the constraints of illness and/or the rigours of onerous treatment. It is also channelled in particular ways by the policies and work processes of the organizations and professionals that provide care. Thus, the activities designed to support patient autonomy also *shape* that autonomy with the (well-intentioned) pressures of organizational and professional culture; it becomes standardized and subject to expectations that reflect organizational and professional priorities and commitment to rational systems. If the very same autonomy can disrupt the genres of clinical work that are designed to support it—if it is *unruly* rather than docile—healthcare professionals can be consoled by the thought that this is also sign of its endurance and perhaps even of its vigour.

Second, patient autonomy is rarely, if ever, the only ethical consideration in play in the context of serious illness. According to the prevailing school of bioethical theory in the United States (Beauchamp and Childress 2013), it is one of four fundamental ethical principles, and any standard bioethical analysis of a case that involved withdrawal of treatment or refusal of consent would include consideration of the other principles. For example, the principle of *non-maleficence* (i.e. the injunction to do no harm) would feature in any standard bioethical analysis of our thought experiment, because actions and decisions that enable suicide would be seen to fall foul of it. Even if this is obvious, it needs to be stated clearly because in order to become part of the routines or genres of clinical work, aspirational models of care need to be simplified, routinized, and standardized, and whilst this might enable their adoption and implementation in typical cases, there will always be a need for judgement when professionals are faced with difficult and/or exceptional cases.

The Limits of Shared Decision-Making

The conclusion we draw about shared decision-making is also a simple one, but we nevertheless think it needs to be made clear. The possibility of shared decision-making exists within limits that are exposed from time to time in the context of high-risk medical procedures. These limits are the points at which the parties to clinical decisions can exercise their autonomy by making *unilateral* decisions. For clinicians, futility determinations are a paradigmatic example and, as our observations suggest, can lead to substantial dissatisfaction among patients and their loved ones. For patients, refusals of care and withdrawals of consent are paradigmatic; again, our observations suggest that these can represent difficult moral quandaries for clinicians. It is no coincidence that these examples feature prominently among sites of legal contestation in medical litigation.

The law currently favours the autonomy of professionals and of patients in each domain of decision-making respectively: ordinarily, patients cannot successfully demand treatment that clinicians refuse to provide, but they can successfully refuse treatment that professionals might seek to force upon them. There are, of course, exceptional cases which the mass media often bring to public notoriety. But refusal of treatment and futility determinations normally enjoy legal protection as zones of unilateral decision-making that border the space within which shared decisions in medicine are currently possible. This is an important contextual constraint in settings where decisions about high-risk procedures are made, and it is important to highlight this because the intuitive ethical appeal of models of care that incorporate shared decision-making as an ideal, such as patient-centred care, can lead to a kind of absolutism in theory and an overzealousness in practice that seeks to implement and sometimes enforce it beyond these limits.

Conclusion

It has been said that sociological research reveals the tension between principles and ideals and actual practice (Bosk 2010). We agree, but we contend that it also shows how ethical principles become embedded in their social context. Both kinds of insight are important. Considered in isolation from their social context, principles and ideals are vulnerable to being dismissed as abstractions whose implications for practice are unclear, notwithstanding any intuitive ethical appeal they might have. This is too often the unfortunate fate of ethically motivated innovations and not only in clinical settings. They are also prone to being pursued as theoretical absolutes and implemented in ways that overreach practical limits. Given this, we need to understand how principles and ideals take hold in a particular context, what the limits are within which they are possible, and what the challenges are that they face. Qualitative research is one path to such understanding. The findings can help to show where the border between the ideal and the real is uneven, where it can be made smoother, and where it is impassable.

Notes

1. For the remainder of this chapter, we will be concerned exclusively with consent for treatment.
2. Sometimes treatment decisions are made by a proxy, on the patient's behalf, as in some of the complex and notorious cases we allude to later in this chapter.
3. Bone marrow transplantation (BMT) can be either *allogeneic* or *autologous*. *Allogeneic* BMT involves storing and transplanting stem cells from a donor. After a suitable donor is identified, the patient undergoes an intensive chemotherapy treatment which destroys the patient's bone marrow, leaving the patient highly vulnerable to infection. Afterwards, the donor's cells are transplanted in a process similar to a blood transfusion, so as to restore the immune system. The chemotherapy is highly toxic and can cause extreme illness, and the patient must remain hospitalized, in isolation, until his or her immune system begins to function again. Thus, the treatment cannot be stopped until the full cycle has been completed. The procedure for *autologous* stem cell reinfusion is similar, except that the patient's own stem cells are harvested, stored, and reinfused.
4. Autologous BMT is sometimes referred to as "high-dose chemotherapy with stem cell rescue."

5. For a more detailed account of the methods of the first study, see Jordens, Montgomery, and Forsyth (2013). For a more detailed account of the methods of the second study, see Little et al. (2008).

6. The case reported by Stein et al. (1998) concerns a thirteen-year-old boy called Jorge who refused an allogeneic BMT for acute lymphocytic leukaemia. It appears in a section of a medical journal reserved for "challenging" cases, with commentaries by two paediatric specialists and a bioethicist. The commentaries call into question the validity of consent: Is a thirteen-year-old sufficiently *capable* of understanding the implications of his decision? And if so, was the patient's *capacity* compromised in this case by depression? The paediatric specialists characterize the patient's decision as "resistance" and conclude that "in many cases, when the resistance is dismantled, the teenage patient may then change his or her mind and consent to treatment" (Robert Wells and Steve Stephenson in Stein et al. 1998, 356). The bioethicist concludes that "whatever efforts are made, in the end, Jorge must accept the treatment willingly. And everyone must accept his decision if he does not" (Lawrence J. Schneiderman in Stein et al. 1998, 357).

7. For a useful interpretive review of the literature on medical futility the reader is referred to Löfmark and Nilstun (2002).

8. Furthermore, accurate and detailed accounts of the experience could actually frighten patients so much that they end up refusing to undergo the procedure, thereby precipitating one of the quandaries we have described earlier.

References

Barry, M.J., F.J. Fowler, A.G. Mulley, and J.V. Henderson. 1995. Patient reactions to a program designed to facilitate patient participation in treatment decisions for benign prostatic hyperplasia. *Medical Care* 33(8): 771–782.

Beauchamp, T., and J. Childress. 1979. *Principles of biomedical ethics*, 1st ed. New York, NY and Oxford: Oxford University Press.

———. 2013. *Principles of biomedical ethics*, 7th ed. New York, NY: Oxford University Press.

Bone Marrow Transplant Network NSW. 2006. *Allogeneic bone marrow transplant: A patient's guide*. Sydney: Bone Marrow Transplant Network NSW.

Bosk, C. 2010. Bioethics, raw and cooked: Extraordinary conflict and everyday practice. *Journal of Health and Social Behavior* 51(Sl): S133–S146.

Christie, F., and J. Martin, eds. 1997. *Genre and institutions: Social processes in the workplace and school*. London and New York, NY: Continuum.

Delbanco, T., D. Berwick, J. Boufford, et al. 2001. Healthcare in a land called People-Power: Nothing about me without me. *Health Expectations* 4(3): 144–150.

DiMatteo, M.R., P. Giordani, H. Lepper, and T. Croghan. 2002. Patient adherence and medical treatment outcomes: A meta-analysis. *Medical Care* 40(9): 794–811.

Ferguson, P., C. Jordens, and N. Gilroy. 2009. Patient and family education in HSCT: Improving awareness of respiratory virus infection and influenza vaccination. A descriptive study and brief intervention. *Bone Marrow Transplantation* 45(4): 656–661.

Flexner, A. 1910. *Medical education in the United States and Canada*. New York, NY: The Carnegie Foundation.

Freidson, E. 1970. *The profession of medicine: A study of the sociology of applied knowledge*. New York, NY: Harper & Row.

Gerteis, M.S., S. Edgman-Levitan, J. Daley, and T. Delbanco. 1993. *Through the patient's eyes: Understanding and promoting patient-centered care.* San Francisco, CA: Jossey-Bass.

Haug, M. 1973. Deprofessionalization: An alternative hypothesis for the future. *The Sociological Review Monograph* 20(S1): 195–211.

Hibbard, J. 2007. Consumer competencies and the use of comparative quality information: It isn't just about literacy. *Medical Care Research and Review* 64(4): 379–394.

Institute of Medicine. 2001. *Crossing the quality chasm: A new health system for the 21st century.* Washington, DC: National Academies Press.

Jones, J. 1981. *Bad blood: The Tuskegee syphilis experiment.* New York, NY: The Free Press.

Jordens, C.F.C., K. Montgomery, and R. Forsyth. 2013. Trouble in the gap: A bioethical and sociological analysis of informed consent for high-risk medical procedures. *Journal of Bioethical Inquiry* 10(1): 67–77.

Kerridge, I.H., M. Lowe, and C. Stewart. 2013. *Ethics and law for the health professions,* 4th ed. Sydney: The Federation Press.

Kite, S., and S. Wilkinson. 2002. Beyond futility: To what extent is the concept of futility useful in clinical decision-making about CPR? *The Lancet Oncology* 3(10): 638–642.

Korsch, B.M. 1989. Current issues in communication research. *Health Communication* 1(1): 5–9.

Little, M., C. Jordens, C. McGrath, et al. 2008. Informed consent and medical ordeal: A qualitative study. *Internal Medicine Journal* 38(8): 624–628.

Löfmark, R., and T. Nilstun. 2002. Conditions and consequences of medical futility: From a literature review to a clinical model. *Journal of Medical Ethics* 28(2): 115–119.

Martin, J.R. 1996. Register and genre: Modelling social context in functional linguistics—narrative genres. *Discourse analysis: Proceedings of the international conference on discourse analysis.* University of Lisbon, Portugal, Colibri/Portuguese Linguistics Association.

Martinez, K., A. Kurian, S. Hawley, and R. Jagsi. 2015. How can we best respect patient autonomy in breast cancer treatment decisions? *Breast Cancer Management* 4(1): 53–64.

McNeill, P. 1993. *The ethics and politics of human experimentation.* Cambridge: Cambridge University Press.

Oppenheim, D., O. Hartmann, A. Ablin, and B. Sourkes. 2002. A child and parent illustrating non-compliance with treatment: Understanding non-compliance with treatment. *Bulletin du Cancer* 89(6): 643–647.

Parsons, T. 1951. Illness and the role of the physicians: A sociological perspective. *American Journal of Psychiatry* 21(3): 452–460.

Roter, D., and J. Hall. 2006. *Doctors talking with patients: Patients talking with doctors.* Westport, CT: Greenwood Publishing Group.

Sadegh-Zadeh, K. 2015. Medical decision-making. In *Handbook of analytic philosophy of medicine,* 2nd ed., edited by K. Sadegh-Zadeh, 699–703. Dordrecht: Springer International Publishing.

Stein, M., R. Wells, S. Stephenson, and L. Schneiderman. 1998. Decision making about medical care in an adolescent with a life-threatening illness. *Developmental and Behavioral Pediatrics* 19(5): 355–358.

3 Off-Label Prescribing

The Borderlands Between Clinical Practice and Experimentation

Narcyz Ghinea, Ian Kerridge, and Wendy Lipworth

Prescribing Medicines Off Label: Physician or Clinical Investigator?

The quandary about off-label prescribing begins with the lack of a decisive definition of the practice. While all definitions of off-label prescribing refer to uses of medicines for indications other than those approved by the regulator, beyond this a vast array of definitions have been used. A systematic review of studies of off-label uses of drugs in paediatrics identified eight different practices defined as "off-label," with different studies rarely utilizing identical definitions (Magalhaes et al. 2015). Examples of off-label uses may include using an approved medicine for a different age group, at a different dose, at a different frequency, or in cases where it is contraindicated.

Recognizing the variety of opinions about what constitutes an "off-label" use of a medicine, Neubert and colleagues undertook a project to establish a consensus definition that could be adopted by regulatory authorities and the scientific community (Neubert et al. 2008). After reviewing literature for different definitions, they asked a panel of scientists, doctors, industry professionals and regulators to vote on definitions of "off-label" use. The definition arrived at defined off-label prescribing in negative terms, as any use that isn't on label:

> All uses of a marketed drug not detailed in the SPC [summary product characteristics], including therapeutic indication, use in age-subsets, appropriate strength (dosage), pharmaceutical form, and route of administration.
> (Neubert et al. 2008, 320)

The considerable variability and ambiguity in definitions of off-label prescribing is exacerbated by the fact that regulators have avoided giving decisive guidance as to when off-label medicines are considered to be "unlicensed," and therefore investigative or experimental. This has significant ramifications, as the prescribing of unlicensed medicines demands stricter criteria are met. Only the U.S. Food and Drug Administration (FDA) has provided any statements on the issue, suggesting that, when the intention is to "practice medicine," no investigational new drug application or review by an institutional review board is necessary (Food and Drug Administration 2014b). At the same time, however, they have declared that drugs used off label may, under some circumstances, be legally interpreted as being unapproved (Food and Drug Administration 2014a). The United Kingdom's General Medical Council has also interpreted certain off-label uses, such as the use of Avastin (bevacizumab) for age-related macular degeneration, to be legally equivalent to an unlicensed use, with the implication that off-label uses of cheaper alternatives to licensed uses are not permitted (Dickson 2015).

Physicians Prescribe Off Label Often and Without "Strong" Evidence

The status of off-label prescribing would not be an issue if the practice was an exception to normal prescribing practices. However, evidence suggests that it is an important component of regular clinical practice. Radley and colleagues' landmark study, published in 2006, analyzed a sample of 150 million prescriptions provided over a single year in the U.S. outpatient setting and found that 21 per cent were off label (Radley, Finkelstein, and Stafford 2006). They also reported that off-label prescribing increases dramatically when using specific classes of medicines, such as cardiac medicines and anticonvulsants.

Off-label prescribing is even more common in certain settings and for certain populations. For instance, in the community setting, more than half of children are prescribed off-label medicines (Chalumeau et al. 2000; Palmaro et al. 2015; Bazzano et al. 2009), whereas in the hospital setting, approximately three-quarters of children receive off-label medicines (Lindell-Osuagwu et al. 2009; Radley, Finkelstein, and Stafford 2006; Czarniak et al. 2015; Ballard et al. 2013; Shah et al. 2007). It has also been shown that off-label use of antipsychotics and anticonvulsants is ubiquitous and most common in the elderly (Weiss et al. 2000; Leslie and Rosenheck 2012; Chen et al. 2006; Kamble et al. 2010; Chen et al. 2005), and anticonvulsants are prescribed off-label up to 80 per cent of the time (Chen et al. 2005, 2006). Evidence also suggests that off-label prescribing is very common during pregnancy (Herring, McManus, and Weeks 2010; Krause et al. 2011) and in treating cancer patients (Soares 2005; Conti et al. 2013; Mellor, Bensted, and Chan 2009; Mellor et al. 2012; Hamel et al. 2015) and that some medicines such as gabapentin and recombinant activated factor VII are used far more often off label than on label (Logan, Yank, and Stafford 2011; Donovan et al. 2013; Radley, Finkelstein, and Stafford 2006; Conti et al. 2013).

Those who have concerns about the prevalence of off-label prescribing observe that the practice is often not "evidence based" according to the usual standards of evidence-based medicine. The study by Radley and colleagues described previously reported that 70 per cent of off-label prescriptions were supported by little or no scientific evidence. Other studies have verified these claims and have also shown that physicians are often not aware that they are prescribing off label (Wong et al. 2017; Chen et al. 2009). This raises important questions about the extent to which off-label prescribing represents non–evidence-based—and therefore experimental—practice, and the very real possibility that physicians may be accused of experimenting (at least according to some definitions), without even realizing that they are doing so.

Methods

There is a relative paucity of qualitative research that focuses on off-label prescribing. One study published in 2016 interviewed seven Belgian hospital-based physicians and six experts in the reimbursement of orphan medicines. The study identified three major justifications for prescribing off label: the medicine is safe and well tolerated, the on-label indication of the medicine is sufficiently general to be extended easily to other uses, and failure of all other evidence-based options (Dooms, Cassiman, and Simoens 2016). Authors of another study, also published in 2016, interviewed twenty-four GPs and six paediatricians in Malta about off-label prescribing in children. This study concluded that the main reason for prescribing off-label was a lack of appropriately licensed medicines. It also noted that medico-legal and safety issues were the principal concern of doctors who prescribed off label (Ellul, Grech, and Attard-Montalto 2016). In 2012, another Canadian study interviewed ten specialists from psychiatry, pain medicine, and neurology to understand why gabapentin was used off label (Fukada et al. 2012). They concluded that where physicians sourced their information appeared to influence their prescribing. Finally, a study published in 2005 investigated attitudes of Scottish GPs towards off-label prescribing to children via a questionnaire circulated to 346 GPs (Ekins-Daukes et al. 2005). The authors concluded the main reasons for prescribing off label included obedience to specialist advice, and lack of licensed alternative medicines.

These studies provide valuable insights into off-label prescribing but focus on a limited range of specialties or even a single medicine. In this research, we sought to contribute to the qualitative literature by conducting interviews with physicians from a wide variety of specialties in order to understand the quandaries faced by physicians when prescribing off label at a more generalizable level. The first author (NG) conducted semi-structured interviews with fourteen physicians practising in nine different specialties including paediatrics (3), obstetrics and gynaecology (3), cardiology (2), general practice (2), mental healthcare (2), oncology (1), rheumatology (1), respiratory medicine (1), and pain management (1). (Two physicians practiced in more than one specialty.) Given that evidence suggests that physicians are often not aware of the fact they are prescribing off label, physicians were prompted to discuss not only off-label prescribing itself but also the other ways in which they determine what is good or bad prescribing, the manner in which they deal with epistemic uncertainty, and how they balance risks and benefits. Sampling was purposive—we were aiming for maximum variation to ensure that no major perspectives were overlooked. The aggregate duration for all interviews was approximately twelve and a half hours, with the average interview duration being approximately fifty-four minutes (interview durations ranged from nineteen minutes through to one hour and twenty-eight minutes). Interviews were recorded and transcribed verbatim. Transcriptions were analyzed using Morse's outline of the cognitive basis of qualitative research (Morse 1994) and Charmaz's outline of data analysis in grounded theory (Charmaz 2006). Interviews were coded paragraph by paragraph, and a coding tree was generated (using XMind 6) from the themes to allow for higher level categorization and conceptualization. Half of the interviews were double coded. Thematic saturation (the point at which no new themes were emerging) was reached after approximately ten interviews. Ethics approval for this research was granted by the University of New South Wales Human Research Ethics Committee (Reference number: 2014–7–20) on 19 May 2014.

Results

Off-Label Prescribing May or May Not Be Experimental

The physicians in this study did not appear to have a clear and consistent conceptualization of what type of prescribing or uses of a medicine may be considered experimental. In addition, whether an off-label use of a medicine may be considered experimental did not consistently depend on either regulatory pronouncements or the strength of available evidence. The picture of experimentation presented by physicians was therefore nuanced, complex, and irreducible to a single definition. Take, for instance, the following quote from a pain specialist describing their own practice of off-label prescribing:

> Well, I think it's obviously an n equals one experiment, but I would generally not regard it as experimental. We would say we'll have a trial of this therapy, and I can see why people would say well isn't that exactly the same thing? But what we are looking for is the evidence that it does work before persisting with it.

In this quotation, two different connotations of the word "experiment" were apparent and led to what appears to be an inherent contradiction. While the physician acknowledged the experimental nature of their prescribing, they nevertheless do not consider themselves to be experimenting because they were actively monitoring the patient to look for any reasons not to continue the therapy.

Another interesting view on what is meant by the term "experimentation" was provided by a general practitioner and dermatologist. In their words:

> I think in some situations, it [i.e. off-label prescribing] would be regarded as experimentation. I think that there are also established practices that are not necessarily approved practices but which are established practices within a body of colleagues who have talked about a particular approach at meetings and conferences or written them up in journals, etcetera. Whilst you still might not have the tick of approval on the product literature for the manufacturer, you've got a body of medical practitioners who still have gathered some informal evidence that it works and have decided as a group that this is not something that's risky or whatever. Where you've got practitioners just doing it de novo, off their own back, for the very, very first time and it's their first random thought, then I think that is experimentation.

According to this quote, experimenting suggests a lack of experience and due diligence on behalf of the prescribing physician and lack of respect for the expert knowledge embodied by the "body of medical practitioners." According to this physician, experimenting has little to do with the regulatory status of the product itself, but rather the capabilities of the practicing physician. A similar view was put forward by a psychiatrist who interpreted "experimental" prescribing in terms of straying from practice accepted as the norm by the medical community and reflected in key reference texts:

> Anything that detracts from that bible [pointing to a key reference text used in the specialty] would probably be, I suppose, experimental.

This was an important observation, as reference texts (e.g. clinical practice guidelines, formularies, and therapeutic manuals and handbooks) often contain off-label uses of medicines, and presumably (in this case), their inclusion in such texts would mean they would no longer be considered "experimental," at least according to the specialty at large.

A gynaecologist who was asked to distinguish between experimentation and conventional clinical practice argued that this distinction depends not just on how much evidence exists in support of the practice but also on whether those results have been verified and whether contradictory evidence exists. In their words:

> Yeah, it's a really good question. And it's a good question because I don't think there is any set answer to it. [Evidence ranges] from one or two RCTs. . . . That's not enough, you know. One study from one group is not enough. What's your cut-off? I think twenty-eight [studies] from twenty-eight different groups is enough, especially when they all say the

same thing. I think if you've got, you know, five or six studies that are giving you conflicting evidence, that's not good enough. But if you—if you've got a group of studies [that confirm each other] . . . then that's really helpful.

While not providing a clear definition of experimentation, this quote is insightful, as it suggests that even practices backed by strong enough evidence to justify registration and market entry may still be considered experimental. Indeed many medicines are approved by regulators with far less evidence than the "one or two RCTs" referred to in this quote, which suggests that not only may off-label medicines not be considered experimental, on-label medicines may, in fact, be considered by physicians to be experimental despite regulatory endorsement.

Taken together, these examples illustrate considerable inconsistency and uncertainty regarding what it is that makes prescribing in general—and off-label prescribing in particular—"experimental." This did not, however, lead to the conclusion that off-label prescribing was reckless or even particularly risky. In the following sections, we demonstrate the various ways that physicians justified practices that may, under some circumstances and according to some definitions, be considered "experimental."

Clinicians Are Experts

The previous quotes demonstrate that the label of "experiment" is not a simple function of the amount of evidence available in support of a clinical decision but that it also depends upon the capabilities of the practicing physician and the norms of the professional group in which the physician practices. One of the ways in which this ambiguity was dealt with was by emphasizing the importance of clinician expertise and of allowing these specialties to make autonomous decisions irrespective of the degree of regulatory endorsement:

So the TGA [Australia's medicines regulator] may have approved a drug for this use, and I would then say, "OK, well, it must be safe to use." But then I wouldn't necessarily be left in the box of what they've said, strictly to be used. I'd look at the evidence for its use and that could work either way. I mean, because there might be very strong evidence for its use in another way than what the TGA said. Likewise, you may not use the medication for the use that—you may not use the medication at all because you feel that the benefit that they are talking about isn't as strong when you look at the trial evidence behind it.

Here, the physician noted that while they take regulatory approval as a signal of a product's safety, they do not necessarily take guidance regarding how the medicine should be used at face value. While some physicians viewed professional guidance as distinct from regulatory endorsement (with the former being much more flexible and realistic in its assessments of medicines), others portrayed the two forms of guidance as being similarly limiting. For example, an emergency paediatrician highlighted how they would not follow official professional guidance if they did not judge it to be the right course of action:

> If I am treating asthma with something and I don't know that there is great evidence that it works. We have guidelines which say that you should give it three times in the first hour for acute asthma. . . . And I often don't, 'cause I don't really think that it helps.

Some physicians took this further, arguing not only that regulatory and professional guidance might be overridden but even that research itself should be questioned:

> Sometimes information is supported by a drug company but I think it's up to the individual to decide the merit of the research. . . . And I think then, it doesn't matter what the research says if you find that the medication is working for your patients. I think that's the proof in the pudding.

These highly sceptical physicians emphasized not only the need to question evidence that exists but also to recognize that absence of evidence of efficacy is not the same as evidence of the absence of efficacy. In this regard, expertise, experience, and due diligence appeared to be far more important as a guide to practice than evidence-based medicine hierarchies that privilege randomized trials over all other forms of evidence:

> Obviously most medicines are not that miraculous or life changing . . . you do have to be prepared to be a bit more flexible because it's just ludicrous to say "oh well, we don't have an RCT in this and this and this. . . . So don't prescribe it because we haven't licensed it for that use." Well [laughs sarcastically] you know.

However, it was recognized that not all physicians have the ability or experience to stray from official guidance. In this regard one physician noted that leveraging expertise should be the domain of only the most senior physicians who have had years to acquire a tacit knowledge of diseases they treat and an understanding of how patients respond to treatment:

> Certainly when you're working in a teaching hospital and you're in a teaching role and you're also in a mentoring role, it's very important to seen to be practising evidence-based medicine because we don't want our younger colleagues to be developing bad habits, you know, if it's

OK for the old man then it must be OK 'cause he says he's seen a case of something that seemed to work. . . . I mean, not only do I have the knowledge by keeping up with the literature and what the literature is saying and what Cochrane is saying and whoever else are saying, but I've also got that long 40 years' experience. And so although I may be primarily guided by evidence-based medicine, I may still sometimes steer a little bit into the anecdotal side of things.

Uncertainty Is Inevitable in Clinical Practice

A second way in which physicians described dealing with the ambiguities regarding the experimental and/or non-evidence-based status of off-label prescribing was by normalizing clinical decisions made in the face of considerable uncertainty. Many participants emphasized that medical research is not a pursuit of certainty but rather involves the reduction and management of uncertainties to acceptable levels. Indeed, setting too high a standard of evidence may, in fact, have the opposite effect to what is intended. As one cardiologist noted:

> To sort of say "well we can't give you anything because there's no evidence" [i.e. strong evidence as defined by the EBM hierarchy] would probably deny some people benefit.

Uncertainty was seen to exist primarily in three forms: uncertainty about the extent to which a medicine is efficacious due to insufficient evidence from randomized controlled trials using clinically meaningful outcome measures, uncertainty about whether and how even those population-level studies that clearly demonstrate efficacy in a trial population will translate to the individual patient, and uncertainty around the diagnosis, and thereby appropriate treatment. An example of the former type of uncertainty was the statement of an obstetrician and gynaecologist who noted that in their specialty, there remained much ambiguity in the evidence base:

> In my field, there are things where we are absolutely crystal clear on issues—not very many of those—but there are certainly really strong good evidence base, lots of randomized trials, fantastic work, crystal clear. Most of it is kind of less clear, a little bit grey. . . . It's the grey zone that's always the problem, isn't it?

With regard to the second type of uncertainty, the aforementioned cardiologist noted:

> And certainly then evidence was really influential in the decisions to prescribe statins, but there are a lot of individual prescribing decisions [i.e. with these same statins] for which there is no real evidence.

With regard to the third type of uncertainty, in some areas of clinical practice, disease categories themselves may be ambiguous.

> I mean, diseases, after all, especially chronic diseases, are really very woolly categories, very woolly categories. The findings, that's easy, a lot of the stuff we see like fatigue for example, or pain, is very woolly. So I think the onus does fall ultimately on the prescriber to be able to rationally justify why that drug was prescribed.

Apart from illustrating that physicians recognize that uncertainty is unavoidable, these quotes also suggest that physicians recognize that the practice of medicine requires a high tolerance of epistemic uncertainty, and therefore an acceptance of practices that may be interpreted as verging on experimental by observers. In this regard, one physician highlighted that evidence does not necessarily drive practice:

> Well, I would have thought that the number of clinical scenarios in which there is level one evidence . . . is sort of no more than 20 per cent of clinical practice and maybe significantly less than that, but it's certainly not driving practice because most of the studies haven't been done.

Medicines Regulation Is a Political Process

A third way in which physicians justified practising in a manner that might be considered experimental was by questioning the social authority of research and regulatory processes. Participants noted that regulators in different jurisdictions might apply different epistemic principles, which effectively leads to medicines (or their uses) remaining "investigational" in one country, while officially endorsed in another. In answer to a question about whether they used medicines that were off label in Australia but on label in other countries, one participant noted, "Yeah—absolutely. Yeah. Yeah. Yeah . . . there's lots of them [that I use]."

Furthermore, participants were alert to the fact that because there is no significant commercial incentive for pharmaceutical companies to seek approval of new medicine uses once the medicine is off patent, labels can rapidly become outdated and cease to accurately reflect current clinical evidence and practice. In this regard, an oncologist and an obstetrician and gynaecologist noted:

> Well, I know plenty of examples . . . [where] the registration studies are so irrelevant to the context in which we're now practising . . . it may not be quite off label but it's certainly not fully on label, as I say.

> In my field there's a lot of stuff that's off label and it's not off label because it's experimental, it's off label because the pharmaceutical company doesn't want to go through the time and expense of having it

approved by the regulator in this country for that indication. . . . If the scientific evidence exists that the drug is effective and safe then it should be regulated for those indications in this country.

So that's another reason where I find the whole TGA [Australia's medicines regulator] process unhelpful because stuff that I'm happy is scientifically sound prescribing is, a lawyer can go "well that was a flake" [since it is not officially on label].

Insofar as medicine licensing depends on evidence, the politics of research also impacts what medicines end up being on or off label.

Now that doesn't mean to say that evidence, level one evidence, isn't regarded as the best evidence, it just means that getting people to agree what's the most important question . . . and then getting the funds to answer that question is not straightforward, shall I say.

Epistemic Justice and Reasonableness

The perceptions that clinicians are experts who should be allowed considerable autonomy, that uncertainty is inevitable in clinical practice, and that regulation is a political—and therefore highly fallible—process were not seen to absolve physicians of the responsibility to make sound prescribing decisions based on rigorous reasoning processes and concern for their patients' best interests. In describing this reasoning, participants invoked a form of epistemic justice, where no form of evidence is dismissed as lacking potential relevance or value. As several participants noted:

I don't look for things, for drugs or medication, therapeutic strategies to be described as weak or strong in evidence. I don't look for that terminology but I do read and I guess there are a couple of sources of information that I might go to if I'm looking up the latest treatment, say, for multiple sclerosis or something like that.

[Sometimes] you have just case reports or small studies which I'm more wary of but depending on what the case is, that can still be very valuable. . . . I don't dismiss things just because they're based on one case.

Well, I think your own experience [is important]—I know if you use a drug and it has an adverse effect, even though it's not considered an adverse effect, and you withdraw the drug and that person gets better and you give the person the drug again and they become unwell, I think it's pretty reasonable evidence.

In this context, the key factor separating a legitimate decision from an illegitimate one appeared to be the ability to defend one's decision. As one participant related:

Somebody was rapping my knuckles one day over me using a certain drug because I actually wanted to use it for its beneficial effect and for its side effects at the same time. . . . I think that physician thought I was going to do something harmful by exploiting the side effects but backed off with that concern when I justified my position.

Defence of prescribing took a variety of forms, including demonstrating that one's reasoning is "logical," "scientific," based on an understanding of pharmacological principles, or more generally makes some "sense."

Well if we have a patient who has a particular issue and there's some not-so-strong evidence that this drug may be effective, then I think we sometimes use these drugs . . . provided that there's some logic behind it.

So follow through a sequence that makes some sense. . . . I would never deliberately set out to use a futile treatment . . . the intention [is always] that there's a reason why I think it might work . . . it needs to be rational, logical, or scientific . . . it's not just "oh I need to give you something, let's open this book and find something."

When you think about it logically, if it's building up somebody's resistance over time to the virus that's causing their problem, then why wouldn't it work?

My pharmacology was still fairly rigorously trained through as a junior doctor, so I'd be expected to know what class of drugs I was prescribing and why. Like, for instance, if I was using a calcium channel antagonist, what was its action and why was I prescribing it?

Discussion

For the practising physicians interviewed, it was evident that there was no clear or consistent distinction to be made between "experimental" and "conventional" practices. This did not, however, cause confusion or paralysis, as physicians utilized their experience and expertise in addressing the inevitable uncertainties that arise as part of clinical practice. While the views of a small number of practitioners should not necessarily be taken at face value, if we take the views of the participants seriously, we find ourselves in the territory of what Mark Tonelli has referred to as "evidence-free medicine" (Tonelli 2009). In using this phrase, Tonelli attempts to redress the imbalance he perceives to result from evidence-based medicine which focuses on categorizing and evaluating the quality of statistical evidence for an intervention, while neglecting the actual decision process by which evidence is translated into practice by physicians in the real world. This is a problem because it valorizes randomized trials and downplays the real ways in which practising physicians interpret and use evidence which is far more holistic and sophisticated than evidence-based models can describe. Indeed, our results showed that physicians recognize that most clinical decisions require expert judgement at some point. If a strict interpretation of EBM [evidence-based medicine] is to be taken seriously, which deems such reasoning as the lowest form of evidence, if a valid form of evidence at all, this would disturbingly imply that all clinical decisions are weakly justified.

Other physicians with philosophical leanings, including Ross Upshur, Miles Little, and Bill Fulford, have likewise argued that clinical decisions are neither driven primarily by statistical evidence from randomized trials nor should they be (Upshur 2014, 2002; Little et al. 2012; Fulford 2014). These commentators remind us of the importance of other explanations and justifications for clinical decisions such as personal experience, physiological reasoning from first principles, and ethical reasoning. In keeping with our participants' view that what ultimately matters is whether a particular practice is defensible, Richard Horton, the Editor-in-Chief of *The Lancet*, has also recognized that the practice of medicine is rhetorical in nature and based upon persuasive argument rather than evidence per se—a paradigm that he has referred to as "interpretive medicine" (Horton 1998). Specifically with respect to off-label prescribing, emerging research suggests that most newly approved clinical indications have arisen not as a result of formal industry-sponsored research but rather as a result of physicians trying to solve clinical problems in practice—in other words, through experts utilizing medicines off label in ways which, at least initially, had little "strong" evidence to support the use (Demonaco, Ali, and Hippel 2006).

Yet despite the numerous justifications for off-label prescribing, regulators and health administrators persist in interpreting "rational" clinical practice through an evidence-based medicine lens. Ghinea and colleagues critique such a view and believe that the purpose of regulatory approval should primarily be to establish initial clinical parameters for newly introduced medicines, not necessarily to provide any specific guidance around acceptable uses (Ghinea et al. 2017). As they state:

> What the label does provide for physicians is perhaps the best systematic assessment of a medicine's approved use at the time of market introduction. Therefore, the label assists with the safe introduction of a new technology into the health system when there may be little other evidence and experience with it. It also ensures there is a minimum level of evidence available about a new medicine for the medical community to work with—particularly relating to safety and efficacy. Indeed a medicine's first registration is perhaps the only point at which society can demand a specific standard of evidence from pharmaceutical companies. We contend this socio-political function of setting the tone around the amount and quality of evidence society expects, in general terms rather than in the details, is perhaps the most important role of the regulatory process. However, this does not mean that the regulator has a special

epistemic or ethical warrant to determine what is, or is not, an appropriate use of a medicine in any particular clinical case—and as our results suggest, this is definitely not the view of the physicians we interviewed.

(Ghinea et al. 2001, 581)

Until such time as this distinction is more widely appreciated, there is a real risk of conflating the position of authoritative institutions about a prescribing practice with the legitimacy of a clinical decision. This can have major implications for practising health professionals, as will be illustrated by two case studies.

Dr John Grygiel and the St Vincent Hospital Under-Dosing Scandal

In February 2016, newspapers in Australia reported that a senior oncologist, Dr John Grygiel, based at St Vincent's Hospital in Sydney, had prescribed head and neck cancer patients "significantly less than the recommended dose of a chemotherapy drug" for up to three years (Peacock 2016, ¶1). The medicine in question was carboplatin, which is widely used to treat a range of cancers. The claim of wrongdoing was linked to the fact that Dr Grygiel had strayed from New South Wales Cancer Institute treatment protocols and had been prescribing all his head and neck cancer patients a dose of 100mgs rather than the usual dose of between 200 and 300mgs. The Director of Cancer Services at St Vincent's Hospital was reported as saying that "I freely admit there's clearly a breakdown in clinical governance," implying that Dr Grygiel had prescribed inappropriately (Peacock 2016, ¶10).

This controversy quickly escalated, with the NSW Ministry of Health conducting an internal inquiry into the matter. The report resulting from the inquiry noted that it was impossible to know if the treated patients would have had different clinical outcomes if they had been given a dosage regimen in accordance with the protocol (NSW Ministry of Health 2016). Nevertheless the report makes the following claim:

> It would be expected that, on a population basis, a failure to adhere to protocols puts every person treated at risk of higher rates of cancer recurrence and higher overall mortality.
>
> (NSW Ministry of Health 2016, Note 58)

In other words, adherence to protocols was deemed a necessary and sufficient measure of good prescribing. Dr Ian Haines, another medical oncologist based at the Alfred Hospital in Melbourne, however, challenged the accusations against Dr Grygiel, noting that there was no evidence that low doses of carboplatin was less effective and that giving lower doses may indeed be beneficial to patients due to lower toxicity (Haines 2016). In the view of Dr Haines, "Shrinking cancers a little bit more with higher and more toxic doses rarely has meaningful benefits for patients." In addition, Dr Haines in his comments alluded to the fact that the culture amongst oncologists was changing, stating that:

The belief that more chemotherapy must be better has underpinned cancer treatment protocols and research for more than 40 years. But we've moved past that.

(Haines 2016, ¶4 under "Why all the confusion?")

While the inquiry into the under-dosing scandal acknowledged the defence that lower doses of carboplatin for head and neck cancer was justifiable on the grounds it reduced toxicities and increased the chance of patients completing treatment, this appeared to be dismissed on the basis there was no evidence to support such claims. The report from the inquiry emphasized the fact the issue was primarily around evidence (NSW Ministry of Health 2016):

No evidence has been presented by Dr Grygiel, or found in the international peer-reviewed literature to support this contention [that a lower dose reduces toxicities and has little disadvantage in terms of efficacy].

(NSW Ministry of Health 2016, Note 61)

Dr Grygiel was interviewed by the Inquiry. At the interview, Dr Grygiel was asked whether he was "aware of any published protocols or guidelines for 100 mg flat dose" to which he replied "no." Further, the practice was not overseen by a Human Research Ethics Committee and no data were collected prospectively nor retrospectively to establish the net effect of this practice on patients' outcomes (benefits and harms).

(NSW Ministry of Health 2016, Note 62)

In the last decade, the protocols for platinum-based chemotherapy in treating people with head and neck cancers have remained unchanged....
There is no perfect way of dosing platinum-based chemotherapy, but the standard remains until a better way is established in accordance with the evidence-generation process described above.

(NSW Ministry of Health 2016, Note 63)

In other words, according to the inquiry, the lack of empirical evidence supporting Dr Grygiel's prescribing meant that his practice was in effect research that had not been approved by a relevant Human Research Ethics Committee. In addition, note 63 appears to suggest that clinical practice should be practised entirely in accordance with what existing statistical evidence permits, even when uncertainty is acknowledged. As a result of Dr Grygiel's actions, his employment with St Vincent's Hospital was terminated and his reputation publicly tarnished (Marchese 2017). While it is impossible to know whether Dr Grygiel's patients were disadvantaged by his decision to stray from conventional clinical practice, it is not at all clear that they were, and it is difficult to know why Dr Grygiel's decision to stray from conventional clinical practice was judged so differently from the myriad other instances of off-label prescribing. The results of discussions with physicians presented earlier in this chapter suggest that many physicians are susceptible to similar accusations insofar as they are prepared to prescribe beyond what is defensible by evidence alone and appear to do so regularly.

The Case of the Off-Label Use of Avastin

Another illustrative case of ambiguity around what constitutes legitimate prescribing was the controversy surrounding the off-label use of Avastin (bevacizumab) for wet age-related macular degeneration (henceforth, wet-AMD). Avastin was first approved by the FDA in 2004 for use in metastatic colorectal cancer. Since that time, its approved indications have expanded to include lung cancer and renal cancer, and it was temporarily approved by the FDA for breast cancer in 2008 before the approval was revoked in 2010.

In 2006 Lucentis (ranibizumab) was approved by the FDA for treatment of wet-AMD. Lucentis is a highly expensive drug costing approximately AU$2,000 per injection. It was reported that in Australia taxpayers spent AU$237 million in 2010 on this drug alone (Lipworth 2011). Astute physicians found a solution to this cost problem. Because Lucentis was a vascular endothelial growth factor (VEGF) inhibitor, and so was Avastin, they reasoned that the latter drug should work for the same condition and could be used for as little as AUD$50 per dose (Lipworth 2011). This clinical reasoning was vindicated by a study published in the *New England Journal of Medicine* in 2011 comparing the two medicines and showing that they were clinically equivalent at one year (The CATT Research Group 2011).

However, Novartis owned both medicines (Novartis shared ownership of Avastin with Roche) and because Avastin would compete directly with Lucentis in the marketplace, Novartis avoided doing the necessary research and avoided seeking regulatory approval for Avastin's use in wet-AMD. Despite a listing of Avastin for wet-AMD never being sought, in 2014, the French government controversially went ahead and listed this off-label use (which in France automatically leads to government subsidy), claiming it would save the government €200 million per annum. In response, the pharmaceutical industry lobby in Europe filed an official complaint with the European Commission, arguing that the French government's actions violated the European Union's approval process and that it "compromises standards of quality, safety and efficacy and could put patients' health at risk" (Wasserman 2015, ¶2). The complaint was ultimately unsuccessful.

In response to this controversy, the United Kingdom's General Medical Council concluded that, while it is illegal to use an "unlicensed drug on grounds of cost if a licensed product is available" it was clear that "a better solution needs to be found for the use of Avastin (bevacizumab) in the treatment of wet age related macular degeneration" (Dickson 2015, ¶3). In addition, the General Medical Council recognized the "invidious position" this controversy placed physicians in. The General Medical Council reached this conclusion despite its recognition elsewhere that "off-label prescribing when there is a licensed alternative routinely occurs in the NHS," and is embedded within NICE guidelines (Cohen 2015b, ¶13 under "GMC guidance"). This scenario raised such consternation and confusion amongst physicians that David Lock QC published what effectively amounted to legal guidance for physicians wishing to prescribe Avastin in the *British Medical Journal* (Lock 2015; Cohen 2015a). According to Lock, there "is nothing to suggest that a doctor who appropriately prescribes bevacizumab for someone with wet-AMD acts in breach of criminal law" and that while physicians should explain to patients that Avastin has not been through the formal testing procedures required to obtain a licence, they are also "entitled to say that the two drugs have been shown to be largely equally effective and that it is better for the NHS generally if the cheaper drug is used" (Lock 2015, under "Could a doctor who prescribes bevacizumab for wet-AMD be sued in negligence?").

This case shows that drug labels can be, and sometimes are, used as a de facto measure of the legitimacy of a prescribing practice. The drug sponsor argued that because Avastin was not on label it was effectively still an investigational drug, and therefore its use would potentially expose patients to unnecessary risks in comparison to the on-label Lucentis. However, as our results have demonstrated, such a narrow view of legitimate clinical practice does not hold up to scrutiny.

Aspiring to "Reasonableness"

In his book *Return to Reason* (Toulmin 2009), the late British philosopher Stephen Toulmin astutely observed:

> Intellectuals in the year 2000 . . . have inherited a family of problems about the idea of Rationality and its relations to those of necessity and certainty. But they tend to ignore the more practical, complementary idea of Reasonableness, or the possibility of living . . . without any absolute necessities or certainties.
>
> (Toulmin 2009, 1)

He continues:

> Before Galileo, Descartes and Hobbes, human adaptability and mathematical rigor were regarded as twin aspects of the human reason. From the 1620s on, this balance was upset, as the prestige of mathematical proofs led philosophers to disown non-formal kinds of human argumentation.
>
> (Toulmin 2009, 14)

It could be argued that evidence-based medicine and the institutions that propagate it, combined with the systematic devaluing of clinical judgement, are a contemporary reflection of this loss of balance within medicine. Informal types of reasoning are considered ambiguous and to be used only in exceptional circumstances when more formal justifications are not available. This bias against clinical and pathophysiological reasoning was explicit at the very inception of evidence-based medicine, which was introduced in *Journal of the American Medical Association* in 1992 as a movement that aimed "to de-emphasise—intuition, unsystematic clinical experience and pathophysiologic rationale as sufficient grounds for clinical decision making" (Evidence-Based Medicine Working Group 1992, 2420). It appears that this imbalance has not only persisted, but also become reified in notions such as "on-label" and "off-label" prescribing. However, as our results demonstrate, the unsystematic, non-formal reasoning that was so derided by early proponents of EBM is the norm rather than the exception. The ubiquity of off-label prescribing in the absence of "strong" evidence as defined by evidence-based medicine hierarchies supports this fact. What this chapter shows is that physicians, and medical professionals at large, need to rediscover the notion of "reasonableness" in clinical practice, and acknowledge that formal distinctions and dichotomies such as "experimental" versus "conventional" treatment, "rational" versus "irrational" prescribing and, indeed, even "evidence-based" versus "non-evidence-based" practice may complicate rather than help achieve the aims of medicine, which is to improve the survival, security, and flourishing of patients. At the same time, ethics committees will need to reconsider how the evaluate research, while health administrators will need to reconsider the role of evidence-based medicine in clinical governance.

References

Ballard, C.D., G.M. Peterson, A.J. Thompson, and S.A. Beggs. 2013. Off-label use of medicines in paediatric inpatients at an Australian teaching hospital. *Journal of Paediatrics and Child Health* 49(1): 38–42.

Bazzano, A.T., R. Mangione-Smith, M. Schonlau, M.J. Suttorp, and R.H. Brook. 2009. Off-label prescribing to children in the United States outpatient setting. *Academic Pediatrics* 9(2): 81–88.

The CATT Research Group. 2011. Ranibizumab and bevacizumab for neovascular age-related macular degeneration. *New England Journal of Medicine* 364: 1897–1908.

Chalumeau, M., J.M. Treluyer, B. Salanave, et al. 2000. Off label and unlicensed drug use among French office based paediatricians. *Archives of Disease in Childhood* 83(6): 502–505.

Charmaz, K. 2006. *Constructing grounded theory: A practical guide through qualitative analysis.* London: Sage Publications.

Chen, D.T., M.K. Wynia, R.M. Moloney, and G.C. Alexander. 2009. U.S. physician knowledge of the FDA-approved indications and evidence base for commonly prescribed drugs: Results of a national survey. *Pharmacoepidemiology and Drug Safety* 18(11): 1094–1100.

Chen, H., A.D. Deshpande, R. Jiang, and B.C. Martin. 2005. An epidemiological investigation of off-label anticonvulsant drug use in the Georgia Medicaid population. *Pharmacoepidemiology and Drug Safety* 14(9): 629–638.

Chen, H., J.H. Reeves, J.E. Fincham, W.K. Kennedy, J.H. Dorfman, and B.C. Martin. 2006. Off-label use of antidepressant, anticonvulsant, and antipsychotic medications among Georgia Medicaid enrollees in 2001. *Journal of Clinical Psychiatry* 67(6): 972–982.

Cohen, D. 2015a. GMC is criticised for refusing to disclose reasons behind its advice to support prescribing for Lucentis rather than Avastin for wet AMD. *British Medical Journal* 350: h1981.

———. 2015b. Why have UK doctors been deterred from prescribing Avastin? *British Medical Journal* 350: h1654.

Conti, R.M., A.C. Bernstein, V.M. Villaflor, R.L. Schilsky, M.B. Rosenthal, and P.B. Bach. 2013. Prevalence of off-label use and spending in 2010 among patent-protected chemotherapies in a population-based cohort of medical oncologists. *Journal of Clinical Oncology* 31(9): 1134–1139.

Czarniak, P., L. Bint, L. Favie, R. Parsons, J. Hughes, and B. Sunderland. 2015. Clinical setting influences off-label and unlicensed prescribing in a paediatric teaching hospital. *PLoS ONE* 10(3): e0120630.

Demonaco, H.J., A. Ali, and E. Hippel. 2006. The major role of clinicians in the discovery of off-label drug therapies. *Pharmacotherapy* 26(3): 323–332.

Dickson, N. 2015. The GMC's stance on Avastin. *British Medical Journal* 350: h2043.

Donovan, P.J., J. Iedema, D.S. McLeod, P. Kubler, and P. Pillans. 2013. Off-label use of recombinant factor VIIa in two tertiary hospitals in Queensland. *ANZ Journal of Surgery* 83(3): 149–154.

Dooms, M., D. Cassiman, and S. Simoens. 2016. Off-label use of orphan medicinal products: A Belgian qualitative study. *Orphanet Journal of Rare Diseases* 11(1): 144.

Ekins-Daukes, S., P.J. Helms, M.W. Taylor, and J.S. McLay. 2005. Off-label prescribing to children: Attitudes and experience of general practitioners. *British Journal of Clinical Pharmacology* 60(2): 145–149.

Ellul, I., V. Grech, and S. Attard-Montalto. 2016. Maltese prescribers use of off-label and unlicensed medicines in children: Perceptions and attitudes. *International Journal of Clinical Pharmacology* 38(4): 788–792.

Evidence-Based Medicine Working Group. 1992. Evidence-based medicine. A new approach to teaching the practice of medicine. *JAMA* 268(17): 2420–2425.

Food and Drug Administration. 2014a. *Guidance for industry: Distributing scientific and medical publications on unapproved new uses—recommended practices (draft).* www.fda.gov/downloads/Drugs/GuidanceComplianceRegulatoryInformation/Guidances/UCM387652.pdf. Accessed January 20, 2018.

———. 2014b. *"Off-label" and investigational use of marketed drugs, biologics, and medical devices—information sheet.* www.fda.gov/RegulatoryInformation/Guidances/ucm126486.htm. Accessed January 20, 2018.

Fukada, C., J.C. Kohler, H. Boon, Z. Austin, and M. Krahn. 2012. Prescribing gabapentin off label: Perspectives from psychiatry, pain and neurology specialists. *Canadian Pharmacists Journal (Ottowa)* 145(6): 280–284.

Fulford, K.W.M. 2014. Values-based practice: The facts. In *Debates in values-based medicines: Arguments for and against*, edited by M. Loughlin, 3–19. Cambridge: Cambridge University Press.

Ghinea, N., I. Kerridge, M. Little, and W. Lipworth. 2017. Challenges to the validity of using medicine labels to categorize clinical behavior: An empirical and normative critique of "off-label" prescribing. *Journal of Evaluation in Clinical Practice* 23(3): 574–581.

Haines, I. 2016. St Vincent's scandal: What's the protocol for chemotherapy and are low doses less effective? *The Conversation*, August 4.

Hamel, S., D.S. McNair, N.J. Birkett, D.R. Mattison, A. Krantis, and D. Krewski. 2015. Off-label use of cancer therapies in women diagnosed with breast cancer in the United States. *SpringerPlus* 4(1): 209.

Herring, C., A. McManus, and A. Weeks. 2010. Off-label prescribing during pregnancy in the UK: An analysis of 18,000 prescriptions in Liverpool Women's Hospital. *International Journal of Pharmacy Practice* 18(4): 226–229.

Horton, R. 1998. The grammar of interpretive medicine. *Canadian Medical Association Journal* 159(3): 245–249.

Kamble, P., J. Sherer, H. Chen, and R. Aparasu. 2010. Off-label use of second-generation antipsychotic agents among elderly nursing home residents. *Psychiatric Services* 61(2): 130–136.

Krause, E., S. Malorgio, A. Kuhn, C. Schmid, M. Baumann, and D. Surbek. 2011. Off-label use of misoprostol for labor induction: A nation-wide survey in Switzerland. *European Journal of Obstetrics and Gynecology and Reproductive Biology* 159(2): 324–328.

Leslie, D.L., and R. Rosenheck. 2012. Off-label use of antipsychotic medications in Medicaid. *American Journal of Managed Care* 18(3): e109–e117.

Lindell-Osuagwu, L., M.J. Korhonen, S. Saano, M. Helin-Tanninen, T. Naaranlahti, and H. Kokki. 2009. Off-label and unlicensed drug prescribing in three paediatric wards in Finland and review of the international literature. *Journal of Clinical Pharmacology and Therapeutics* 34(3): 277–287.

Lipworth, W. 2011. Counting the cost of off-label prescribing. *MJA Insight*, June 27.

Little, M., W. Lipworth, J. Gordon, P. Markham, and I. Kerridge. 2012. Values-based medicine and modest foundationalism. *Journal of Evaluation in Clinical Practice* 18(5): 1020–1026.

Lock, D. 2015. Avastin and Lucentis: A guide through the legal maze. *British Medical Journal* 350: h1377.

Logan, A.C., V. Yank, and R.S. Stafford. 2011. Off-label use of recombinant factor VIIa in U.S. hospitals: Analysis of hospital records. *Annals of Internal Medicine* 154(8): 516–522.

Magalhaes, J., A.T. Rodrigues, F. Roque, A. Figueiras, A. Falcao, and M.T. Herdeiro. 2015. Use of off-label and unlicenced drugs in hospitalised paediatric patients: A systematic review. *European Journal of Clinical Pharmacology* 71(1): 1–13.

Marchese, D. 2017. Chemotherapy dosage controversy: Doctor John Grygiel settles unfair dismissal case. *ABC News*, March 24.

Mellor, J.D., K.E. Bensted, and P.L. Chan. 2009. Off label and unlicensed prescribing in a specialist oncology center in Australia. *Asia Pacific Journal of Clinical Oncology* 5(4): 242–246.

Mellor, J.D., P. Van Koeverden, S.W. Yip, A. Thakerar, S.W. Kirsa, and M. Michael. 2012. Access to anticancer drugs: Many evidence-based treatments are off-label and unfunded by the Pharmaceutical Benefits Scheme. *Internal Medicine Journal* 42(11): 1224–1229.

Morse, J.M. 1994. "Emerging from the data": The cognitive process of analysis in qualitative inquiry. In *Critical issues in qualitative research methods*, edited by J.M. Morse, 23–43. Thousand Oaks, CA: Sage Publications.

Neubert, A., I.C. Wong, A. Bonifazi, et al. 2008. Defining off-label and unlicensed use of medicines for children: Results of a Delphi survey. *Pharmacological Research* 58(5–6): 316–322.

NSW Ministry of Health. 2016. *Inquiry under section 122 of the Health Services Act 1997: Off-protocol prescribing of chemotherapy for head and neck cancers.* www.health.nsw.gov.au/patients/cancertreatment/pages/cancer-patients-inquiry. aspx. Accessed January 20, 2018.

Palmaro, A., R. Bissuel, N. Renaud, et al. 2015. Off-label prescribing in pediatric outpatients. *Pediatrics* 135(1): 49–58.

Peacock, M. 2016. Up to seventy cancer patients given wrong dose for three years at Sydney's St Vincent's Hospital. *ABC News*, February 19.

Radley, D.C., S.N. Finkelstein, and R.S. Stafford. 2006. Off-label prescribing among office-based physicians. *Archives of Internal Medicine* 166(9): 1021–1026.

Shah, S.S., M. Hall, D.M. Goodman, et al. 2007. Off-label drug use in hospitalized children. *Archives of Pediatrics and Adolescent Medicine* 161(3): 282–290.

Soares, M. 2005. "Off-label" indications for oncology drug use and drug compendia: History and current status. *Journal of Oncology Practice* 1(3): 102–105.

Tonelli, M.R. 2009. Evidence-free medicine: Forgoing evidence in clinical decision making. *Perspectives in Biology and Medicine* 52(2): 319–331.

Toulmin, S. 2009. *Return to reason.* Cambridge, MA: Harvard University Press.

Upshur, R. 2002. If not evidence, then what? Or does medicine really need a base? *Journal of Evaluation in Clinical Practicing* 8(2): 113–119.

———. 2014. Does medicine need a base? A critique of modest foundationalism. In *Debates in values-based practice: Arguments for and against*, edited by M. Loughlin. Cambridge: Cambridge University Press.

Wasserman, E. 2015. European pharma lobby says "non" to French funding for off-label Avastin. *FiercePharma*, September 2.

Weiss, E., M. Hummer, D. Koller, H. Ulmer, and W.W. Fleischhacker. 2000. Off-label use of antipsychotic drugs. *Journal of Clinical Psychopharmacology* 20(6): 695–698.

Wong, J., A. Motulsky, M. Abrahamowicz, T. Eguale, D.L. Buckeridge, and R. Tamblyn. 2017. Off-label indications for antidepressants in primary care: Descriptive study of prescriptions from an indication based electronic prescribing system. *British Medical Journal* 356: j603.

4 Clinical Quandaries Associated With Accelerated Access to Medicines

Jessica Pace, Narcyz Ghinea, Miriam Wiersma, Bronwen Morrell, Ian Kerridge, and Wendy Lipworth

Introduction

Medicines can save and improve lives, but they can also be very expensive, in terms of both overall and unit costs. It is not uncommon for new therapies (such as biological agents and targeted therapies used to treat conditions such as cancer, hepatitis, and autoimmune diseases) to cost upward of US$100,000 per patient per year of treatment. The prices of the direct-acting antivirals for the treatment of hepatitis C have made headlines around the world. One example is sofosbuvir (marketed as Sovaldi), with an initial price of US$1,000/tablet (or $84,000 for a three-month course) (Ghinea et al. 2017; Dore and Martinello 2016). Similarly, the CAR-T gene therapy agent tisagenlecleucel (Kymriah) for the treatment of paediatric and young adult acute lymphoblastic leukaemia (approved by the U.S. Food and Drug Administration in August 2017) costs US$475,000 for a one-time infusion (Bach, Giralt, and Saltz 2017), while eculizumab (Soliris) for the treatment of the rare diseases paroxysmal nocturnal haemoglobinuria (PNH) and atypical haemolytic uremic syndrome (aHUS) costs approximately US$500,000 per patient per year of treatment and is one of the world's most expensive drugs (Crowe 2017). Collectively, expenditure on pharmaceuticals accounted for US$322 billion in the United States in 2015 (Centers for Disease Control and Prevention 2017), €200 billion in the European Union in 2014 (OECD 2016), and AU$17.1 billion in Australia in 2014 (OECD 2017; Health Services Research Association of Australia and New Zealand 2016); accounting for 2 per cent, 1.4 per cent, and 1.3 per cent of GDP, respectively (OECD 2017). It is predicted that these costs will increase substantially in the near future due to factors such as the ongoing development of targeted biological agents (whose complex manufacturing, storage, and administration processes result in high unit costs), ageing populations with greater medical needs and an associated rise in chronic conditions, and the emergence of new healthcare markets in the developing world increasing the demand for expensive pharmaceuticals (Pace, Pearson, and Lipworth 2015).

The high cost of many therapies means that, in practice, some form of subsidy—either public or private—is needed before all but the wealthiest patients can access these new treatments. However, decisions about subsidizing expensive medicines occur in the context of escalating healthcare costs and budget constraints, meaning that it is impossible for any payer to provide all patients with access to all medicines. Inevitably, some patients will miss out on treatment that they want or need.

The realities of healthcare funding have led to increasing calls for physicians to act as stewards of scarce healthcare resources. The idea here is that payers will have more resources to distribute if physicians make "rational" decisions about which medicines to prescribe for which patients. For example, the American Board of Internal Medicine (ABIM) Foundation, American College of Physicians and European Federation of Internal Medicine's "Medical Professionalism in the New Millennium: A Physician Charter" (ABIM Foundation, ACP-ASIM Foundation, and European Federation of Internal Medicine 2002) reinforces a physician's commitment to a "just distribution of finite resources" as an essential aspect of medical professionalism. The Australian Medical Association (AMA) Code of Ethics requires physicians to "practise effective stewardship, the avoidance or elimination of wasteful expenditure in healthcare, in order to maximise quality of care and protect patients from harm while ensuring affordable care in the future" (Australian Medical Association 2016, 6). The Australian Medical Board Code of Conduct for Doctors in Australia (Medical Board of Australia 2014) also notes that "it is important to use healthcare resources wisely" and that good medical practice involves "supporting the transparent and equitable allocation of resources" and "understanding that your use of resources can affect the access other patients have to healthcare resources" (Medical Board of Australia 2014, 17).

There have also been recent moves, particularly in the United States, towards payment systems based on the quality of care provided and improvement in outcomes achieved rather than on the volume of care (Jordens 2000); these are termed "value-based payments" and are one tool available to Accountable Care Organizations (ACOs) (Paige 2015). The aims of such programmes are two-fold—both to increase the quality of care provided to individual patients and to decrease overall healthcare costs (Chee et al. 2016). The U.S. Centers for Medicare and Medicaid Services (CMS) set a goal of 50 per cent of Medicare payments being in value-based arrangements by 2018, and private insurers are quickly following suit (Paige 2015; Chee et al. 2016). Meanwhile, a recent OECD report found that a range of healthcare systems—including those in France, Germany, the United Kingdom, Brazil, Korea, Australia, and New Zealand—had utilized value-based payment systems (Cashin et al. 2014).

Despite these moves, it is almost universally accepted that a physician's duty of care is, first and foremost, to the individual patient. For example, the United Kingdom's General Medical Council in their Good Medical Practice code urges doctors to make the care of their patient their first concern (Medical Board of Australia 2014). The ABIM Foundation, American College of

Physicians, and European Federation of Internal Medicine's "Medical Professionalism in the New Millennium: A Physician Charter" (ABIM Foundation, ACP-ASIM Foundation, European Federation of Internal Medicine 2002) similarly emphasizes the primacy of patient welfare, whereas the Australian Medical Association (AMA) Code of Ethics for doctors tells doctors to "consider first the well-being of your patient" (Australian Medical Association 2016, 1) and the Australian Medical Board Code of Conduct notes that "the care of [a physician's] patient is their primary concern" (Medical Board of Australia 2014, 5).

It is, of course, unsurprising that both historical codes and more contemporary statements about professionalism emphasize the primacy of the patient and the physician's obligation to promote the patient's best interests, as these codes and statements arise from the clinical space and so emphasize the clinical dyad. It is similarly unsurprising that statements about reduction of waste and rational prescribing represent the interests and perspectives of their "authors" (i.e. government, health services, and pharmaceutical policy bodies) whose primary concern is not the welfare of the individual patient or the agency of the individual practitioner but the functioning of the healthcare system and needs of the broader population.

While it is quite possible that stakeholders can navigate both sets of values with ease by knowing where their primary interests lie within any given role, there are clearly situations where a physician's duty to the individual patient will be in tension with their responsibilities to the broader community to use healthcare resources wisely. In some of these situations, the decision to prescribe a drug will clearly be socially irresponsible, for example, prescribing a drug that is unlikely to work and/or is much more expensive than alternative treatment options because a patient wishes to try it. In other cases, it will not be as obvious that a decision is socially irresponsible—for example, where a drug is massively expensive but also effective, and there are no other cheaper alternatives or when a drug is not cost-effective but still better for the patient than a much cheaper and slightly inferior alternative. In either case, however, the physician may find that their desire to advocate for a patient is at odds with their perceived responsibilities to the community.

These kinds of tensions have long been recognized and have been examined at both the macro and micro levels. At the macro level, sociologists have explored what the doctor's professional role entails and whether doctors have the necessary competence to make decisions about—or even with consideration of—resource allocation (Jordens 2000; Tilburt 2014; Huddle 2005, 2011, 2013, 2014). They have also examined changing consumer expectations, including, for example, whether patients want doctors to decide on issues such as resource allocation and cost containment when making clinical decisions (e.g. prescribing medicines) and, if so, what doctors need to know and be able to do in order to perform this role. At the micro level, the focus of sociological inquiry has been on how physicians manage their competing roles through concepts such as power, rationing, and resource dependency (Light and Hughes 2001; Montgomery and Schneller 2007).

Within the ethics literature, there are long-standing debates about what the doctor's role should be and whether it is appropriate for them to make clinical decisions with resource allocation in mind. Those in favour argue that the healthcare system in which doctors practice influences the quality of care that they can provide and that by focusing on the promotion of social justice, just distribution of resources, and fair access to care, the health of all patients can be improved (Kopelman 1999; Pellegrino 1986). However, others argue that allowing doctors to consider resource allocation when making clinical decisions interferes with their primary duties to their individual patients and could result in decisions guided by values that are not shared by the broader community (Veatch 1990, 2009, 2012). An interesting new research programme led by Siun Gallagher is examining the experiences and values of physicians towards involvement in supraclinical advocacy (including the group of activities focused on macro-level priority setting) (see Chapter 6 in this volume; Gallagher and Little 2017).

Despite these reflections on the physician's role in resource allocation, there remains little agreement on the best way for physicians to navigate the associated tensions. This is significant because such tensions are likely only to grow, not only because medicines are becoming more expensive, but also because there are growing calls from patients, their advocates, and the pharmaceutical industry for earlier access to more new medicines. These calls have been prompted by concerns that current regulatory and reimbursement processes are too cumbersome and too rigid in terms of evidence and cost-effectiveness thresholds—particularly when patients have limited treatment options or life expectancy—and take a number of forms. The pharmaceutical industry and industry-funded consumer groups encourage patients to demand "access to timely and affordable medicines" (Cancer Drugs Alliance 2018) and advocate for the "right to try" experimental therapies without the usual regulatory oversight (Goldhill 2015). Politicians around the globe have also pledged to facilitate faster access to new therapies. For example, former U.S. Vice President Joe Biden committed to hastening the approval of promising new cancer drug combinations (Hirschler 2016) while U.S. President Donald Trump vowed to deregulate the drug industry "at a level that nobody's ever seen before" in order to address what he described as the U.S. Food and Drug Administration's (FDA) "slow and burdensome" regulatory approval processes (Kaplan 2017, ¶1). Meanwhile, in countries with publicly funded insurance programmes, politicians appeal to voters by promising to provide funding for specific medicines that have been rejected by public or private insurers; one example is the commitment by the New Zealand opposition Labour party to fund pembrolizumab (Keytruda) for the treatment of melanoma after it was rejected by that country's public payer (PHARMAC) (Edwards 2016). Additionally, as of January 2018, thirty-eight U.S. states have passed "Right to Try" legislation, allowing patients to request access to unapproved therapies without the need for FDA approval (Joffe and Lynch 2018). Finally, a number of recent inquiries—including the U.K. Government's Accelerated Access Review (Accelerated Access Review: Final Report 2017), the Australian Government Expert Review of Medicines and Medical Devices Regulation (Sansom, Delaat, and Horvath 2015), and the Australian Senate Inquiry into the Availability of New, Innovative and Specialist Cancer Drugs in Australia (Australian Senate Community Affairs Reference Committee 2015)—have critiqued existing regulatory and reimbursement systems for not providing patients with timely access to new therapies.

Calls for earlier access to medicines based on lower standards of evidence have been particularly acute when it comes to cancer medicines, despite the high price and varying effectiveness of many new cancer therapies. While some new cancer therapies have proven to be very effective—for example, imatinib (Gleevec) for the treatment of chronic myeloid leukaemia (CML) has been described as a miracle drug, with five-year survival rates improving from 30 per cent before the drug was introduced in 2001 to almost 90 per cent in 2006 (Pray 2008)—a number of recent studies (Davis et al. 2017; Fojo, Mailankody, and Lo 2014; Kim and Prasad 2015; Rupp and Zuckerman 2017; Banzi et al. 2015) have shown that for many other cancer medicines, their effects on survival are either minimal (extending life by weeks or months at most) or unknown. This heightens the tensions that clinicians may face, as their competing responsibilities to the individual patient and the broader community become more difficult to reconcile and the consequences of not fulfilling a particular duty more serious.

In this chapter, we report the results of a qualitative study in which Australian physicians involved in the prescription of high cost cancer medicines describe their approaches to navigating the tensions that arise when prescribing these therapies, in the context of demands for accelerated access. Our research questions were:

1   What duties do physicians identify as important when prescribing high-cost cancer medicines?
2   Are there tensions between these duties and, if so, how do physicians navigate these?

Empirical Observations

Study Setting

The Australian healthcare system is complex, with responsibilities split between different levels of government and the public and private sectors. The main funder of healthcare in Australia is the federal government through its universal health insurance scheme known as Medicare. This is funded through the taxation system and provides free or subsidized access to both medical services through the Medical Benefits Schedule (MBS) and pharmaceuticals through the Pharmaceutical Benefits Scheme (PBS). Although not compulsory, private health insurance is available for those who wish to fully or partly cover the costs of treatments not covered by Medicare.

Australia has a two-stage system to provide access to pharmaceuticals (Gallego, Taylor, and Brien 2007). Before a medicine can be marketed, it must first be evaluated for quality, safety, and efficacy by the Therapeutic Goods Administration (TGA; Australia's regulatory agency). The Advisory Committee on Prescription Medicines (ACPM) advises the TGA on whether a product should be registered for use. Once a medicine has been registered by the TGA, the manufacturer can then apply to have it listed on the Pharmaceutical Benefits Scheme (PBS) in order to facilitate patient access in the outpatient setting (the majority of medicines for inpatients are funded through hospital budgets). The Pharmaceutical Benefits Advisory Committee (PBAC) assesses all applications for listing and makes recommendations to the Commonwealth Minister for Health about which medications should be subsidized. In making an assessment, the PBAC considers the safety, efficacy, cost-effectiveness, and estimated budget impact of the medicine as well as the quality of supporting evidence for each of these factors. If a medicine is listed on the PBS, patients pay up to a specified co-payment each time the medicine is dispensed (in 2018, this was $39.50, reduced to $6.40 for people receiving income support payments) (Department of Health 2018). If the medicine is registered by the TGA but not listed on the PBS, it can still be prescribed; however, patients need to find other ways to cover the cost of the drug. Potential options include funding through public hospital drug and therapeutics committees (DTC), industry compassionate access schemes, private health insurance, or personal fund-raising (Gallego, Taylor, and Brien 2007).

Methods

We conducted sixteen interviews with physicians who had a background in oncology or haematology. Participants were recruited using a combination of sampling methods, including convenience and snowball sampling and unsolicited emails to experts with relevant professional backgrounds. Semi-structured interviews were conducted by NG (either by phone or face to face) and lasted between sixty and ninety minutes each. Interviews focused on four major "themes" that have emerged in debates about the provision of "early" access to innovative cancer medicines (identified in our previous work, see Ghinea, Lipworth, and Little 2017): the need to support innovation, the need to show compassion, the importance of not leaving anyone behind, and the need to maintain a sustainable health budget. Interviews elaborated on these themes by challenging participants' commitment to each theme through exploration of the consequences of following each one to its logical conclusion.

An inductive approach—informed by Morse's (1994) outline of the cognitive basis of qualitative research and Charmaz's (2006) outline of data analysis in grounded theory—was taken to data analysis. This involved initial coding via line-by-line analysis, synthesis of codes into categories, focused coding using these categories, and abstraction into analytic concepts. A process of constant comparison was used, with continual refinement and enrichment of codes. Data analysis continued until categories were saturated (i.e. all codes appeared to fit under one or more of the existing categories and all concepts were fully described and well understood). Emergent material was then arranged to answer the research questions. All interviews were analyzed and thematic saturation was reached after approximately ten interviews. Transcripts were cross-coded by JP, MW, and NG, with detailed discussion used to ensure consistency in emergent codes, categories, and concepts. Importantly, we did not enter into the research process with any expectations that physicians would describe tensions related to resource allocation. This emerged only after we had analyzed the interviews and the categories and concepts were developed from the data.

Interviews were recorded (with the participants' permission) and transcribed verbatim. The study was approved by the University of Sydney's research ethics committee (protocol number 2015/11). All participants were emailed participant information statements and consent forms as part of the invitation to participate and provided either signed consent forms or recorded verbal consent prior to commencing the interview.

Results

Physicians identified two sets of competing duties that arose when prescribing high-cost cancer medicines. First, they emphasized the need to simultaneously (1) provide patients with hope and compassionate care and (2) protect them by making decisions that are based on evidence of efficacy and safety (i.e. a tension within the physician role). Second, they felt the need to both (1) advocate for patients and (2) protect scarce healthcare resources for the good of the broader community (a tension between two competing roles). Physicians described the actual or potential difficulties of navigating these tensions and suggested some strategies to assist with this task, namely, disaggregating their roles and responsibilities, deferring to experts and policymakers, and finding alternative ways for patients to gain access to high cost medicines—each of which provides a potential means for preventing and managing cognitive dissonance.

Duties to Patients

THE IMPORTANCE OF PROVIDING HOPE AND COMPASSIONATE CARE

All participants noted that providing compassionate care and hope to patients were key parts of their role as a physician. Compassionate care can include providing patients in desperate situations—such as those with limited life expectancy and few treatment options—with access to medicines that are known to have only small or negligible impacts on survival and/or quality of life, as these are meaningful to patients (e.g. by allowing them to spend less time in hospital or to continue participating in everyday activities):

> [I]t's not always just about a cure, it can also be about . . . significant remission time . . . [so people can live] with the cancer as opposed to dying from it . . . from an organizational point of view if there is evidence there that this drug will make a difference to the life of a patient, then we feel that there should be access to that drug. Then you've got the other argument . . . [i.e.] well there's nothing for me therefore I just want access to this drug because it might work.

The duty to provide hope was taken equally seriously and was seen to persist at all stages of a patient's disease, even though what a patient could realistically hope for may change as their disease progressed:

> Hope is incredibly important and don't get me wrong I'm not a tight arsed narky person. We always have hope, we sometimes change what we're hoping for, but we always have hope.

THE IMPORTANCE OF PROTECTING PATIENTS BY MAKING DECISIONS
BASED ON EVIDENCE

While participants emphasized the importance of providing patients with compassionate care and with hope, they noted that this alone was an insufficient basis to make therapies available to patients. They cautioned against providing patients with "false hope" and emphasized that any treatment offered to patients should have reasonable evidence of benefit:

> The thing about hope is that it needs to be backed up with some reasonable evidence, and if you are providing false hope to patients I'm not sure that you are doing them very many favours.

In keeping with this view, several participants argued that, when discussing potential treatment options with patients, it is important to be realistic about the chance that they will benefit and to discuss the availability of alternative treatment options, such as palliative care, in order for patients to make an informed treatment choice:

> [T]here should be no false hopes, you ought to be able to say well you've got a 10 per cent chance of responding to this drug. And so the alternative is palliative medicine, in other words, pain control and good symptom control and spending time with your family. . . . So I think it's an informed choice, plus it's important that the doctor doesn't provide

false hope by saying "oh the chance of responding is 60–70 per cent" where they're not.

They noted a tension between the emotional drive to provide patients with hope and compassionate care on the one hand and with evidence-based (i.e. efficacious and safe) care on the other:

> I think the issue that I would emphasize is you can't get away from the evidence, you've got to make sure that there's evidence there. The idea that we, here's a new drug, it might work, and therefore the emotion is that we should immediately grab it, well you know I think patients are more important than that. I do think we have an obligation to them to see if there's evidence there that it's going to work.

Duties to the Broader Community

THE IMPORTANCE OF PROTECTING RESOURCES

Most participants emphasized the importance of considering the costs and opportunity costs of the medicines that they prescribe and achieving an appropriate balance between thinking about the sustainability of the health-care system overall and ensuring that individual patient needs are met:

> Because there is a public health issue here as well, which we have to very finely balance. If we spend $100,000 a year on a drug for a single person, we can't spend $5,000 a year on a drug for twenty people. And we do have to balance that as a public sector. I work in the public system, so I think not just about my own intention but the impact of my decisions on the public health dollar. Now I imagine that is completely out of step with most private practicing oncologists and possibly even most public practicing oncologists, it's just that actually you do have to take the bigger view.

The need to protect resources was seen as a reason to withhold treatment from patients, even if this conflicted with the desire to offer hope and compassionate care:

> The government have to set a condition about cost benefits, and you cannot argue that it doesn't matter if it works or not, it gives the patient hope. I think if you gave me $140,000 I could give hope to patients in all sorts of different ways, and I can do it for a lot less money.

> I think if we get too driven by compassion and patient advocacy . . . there'll be a disparity between say what gets funded for breast cancer, compared to what gets funded for some extremely rare cancers.

Several participants also emphasized that they were not just doctors but also taxpayers contributing to the funding of new cancer medicines, and therefore had a duty to protect scarce healthcare resources by advocating for their appropriate use. They argued that this duty was heightened by the high price of many new therapies and the fact that many agents are used for long periods of time (rather than a short course as was the case with many agents in the past):

> [I]t's also my responsibility to be pushing back, particularly as these agents are not six months' worth of therapy and then stop—they're continuous. . . . And I as a taxpayer feel very strongly that we have a responsibility to be advocating for the appropriate use of these innovative agents, particularly when they come at such a high cost.

A key tension identified by the physicians in this study was, therefore, that of prioritizing the needs and desires of individual patients versus protecting population health resources:

> On the one hand, we've got a responsibility to the broader community to spend the health dollar wisely, and there's only so much money in the pot, and if you're going to put all your money into enzyme treatment for Gaucher's disease or something, then you're not going to be able to fund Ibrutinib. And incidentally you're not going to be able to fund roads and schools and everything else either and repairing the Barrier Reef. So there's only so much money. On the other hand, in the clinic that goes out the window, because across the table from you is someone in a desperate situation, and that person has to be your top priority. So we're often in these situations of extreme conflict.

There were, therefore, two key tensions faced by physicians:

1 The desire to provide hope and compassionate care to individual patients versus the desire to provide these patients with evidence-based (i.e. efficacious and safe) care.
2 The desire to provide hope and compassionate care to individual patients versus the desire to protect community resources.

Managing Tensions

Physicians described three main approaches to managing these tensions: preventing cognitive dissonance by disaggregating roles and deferring to experts and policymakers, experiencing and managing their own cognitive dissonance, and finding alternative ways for patients to access medicine (which can be a means of both preventing and managing cognitive dissonance).

Some physicians appeared to navigate these tensions relatively comfortably. For these participants, disaggregating their roles and responsibilities and/or deferring to experts, including hospital-based high-cost drug committees, institutional or departmental policymakers, and health economists who make these decisions at a "population" level (be that the hospital, health district, or state), was an important strategy. This strategy allowed them to advocate strongly for their patient to have access to a particular drug but also admit that they do not have the power to make that decision and must respect both the decision that is made (whatever this is) and the decision-making process:

> So I have to be guided there by the smart health economists who make calculations based on the economic worth of an individual's productive year of life and accept that that's a horrible reality and see that it comes in somewhere around the $60,000 to $70,000 productive year of life year earned. But I have enormous difficulty with that concept as a clinician and as a parent and spouse. I couldn't possibly even begin to imagine applying those statistics in that situation, as I guess nobody could.

Many lamented the fact that many stakeholders appear to advocate for new therapies to be funded without adequate consideration of their safety, efficacy, or cost-effectiveness and appreciated the existence of an impartial body such as Australia's PBAC that makes an assessment of the value of new drugs based solely on factors such as effectiveness, toxicity, cost-effectiveness, and sustainability:

> So while it's perfectly OK to talk about patient impact, and it's perfectly OK to have different input, you do need a rigorous non-emotional system that is able to say no and that can withstand the emotional pleas. Because otherwise we'll bankrupt the country.

Importantly, the view that health technology assessment agencies should restrict access to medicines was not seen to be incompatible with taking seriously the need to provide patients with hope. For example, one participant suggested that funders could embark on risk-sharing arrangements with pharmaceutical companies in order to "put a price on hope," whereas another argued for "measured compassion" on the part of those making resource allocation decisions:

> There has to be measured compassion in some sense, because things can get a little bit out of hand, where a patient demands a bone marrow transplant for kidney cancer, which although it has been done, doesn't actually help anybody, and then they suggested that's what they need.

And based on some relatively flimsy old evidence and you try and use compassion argument to make the government pay for whatever, a drug or something, for the cancer. So I think the compassion has to be measured.

While participants were, for the most part, very protective of Australia's PBAC and its capacity to restrict access to medicines, they did note that there were certain situations where it may be appropriate to revise current evidence standards, for example, when it comes to the funding of medicines for rare cancers or for use at the end of life:

> I think there is, and particularly medicines around the end of life and how you define that could be argued, drugs where life expectancy of less than twelve months or two years. I think there should be greater leeway in terms of the thresholds that have to be met to actually fund drugs.

Even in these cases, however, the majority of participants were happy to leave payers in control of access to medicines—that is, they did not advocate for *all* medicines being available at the discretion of physicians alone. Indeed, some participants advocated for *increased* regulation to assist physicians in managing this tension.

EXPERIENCING AND MANAGING THEIR OWN COGNITIVE DISSONANCE

While some participants were able to avoid cognitive dissonance by deferring to population-level decision-makers, others described considerable distress associated with what they perceived to be serious personal quandaries:

> So if you look, so as doctors if you look at the patient/doctor interaction, as doctors we need to be advocating the best we can for the patient who is in front of you. And that is our role in that relationship. . . . And so there's all this emotional drive and stuff. But on the other hand, the money has got to come from somewhere, and what are you going to stop doing?

One way that participants had of making sense of this dissonance was to consider the situation from a range of perspectives—the patient and their family, the prescribing clinician, and the taxpayer—as a means of understanding the different interests at play (even though they may not agree with all of these):

> I think it's very easy for me to say as the prescribing clinician to sit here and say I completely understand. And I do, because I not only want the PBS to pay for this expensive therapy, I want them to pay for the next expensive therapy too. So on a population perspective I completely

understand that. Explaining that to the patient in front of you, or if it was actually me sitting there waiting for that medication to become available, I'd have a very different perspective on it. And I think that's obvious.

I have a view as a hopefully educated citizen and a view as a clinician, and they're not necessarily concordant, because of the conflicting priorities that you have. If I go down the path of conjuring into my brain a series of my current patients and I advocate for them, their lives are priceless. They are young adults, they have young children, even two years of life for these people can see a child graduate, a child marry, two grandchildren born, you know these are priceless life events for anybody. So then I have to translate myself to being an educated citizen and trying to be cool and cold and calm and collected about that. And you realize that there isn't an endless money tree.

Understanding these different perspectives did not, however, always enable physicians to avoid difficult situations in which "dichotomous" values came into conflict:

This is a very difficult one, and I don't think it's possible to reconcile this dichotomous situation where we find ourselves in, sometimes simultaneously.

FINDING ALTERNATIVE WAYS OF FACILITATING ACCESS

Finally, participants emphasized the importance of considering alternative ways to facilitate access to new cancer medicines, which can be both a means of managing and preventing cognitive dissonance. These included encouraging clinical trials, addressing high drug prices which are an important barrier to access, leveraging industry compassionate access programmes, utilizing managed entry programmes, and implementing special funds separate to the usual budget; each has its own advantages and disadvantages.

Encouraging Clinical Trials   For many participants, the best way to provide hope and compassionate care to patients, while still minimizing harm to individuals and health systems, was to enrol patients in clinical trials. They emphasized that rather than payers (in this case, the federal government) spending money on treatments whose efficacy is still largely unknown, a better option would be to invest in clinical trials infrastructure and to encourage the conduct of clinical trials in Australia in order to provide patients with faster access to new cancer therapies:

And I appreciate that it's important patients have hope and want to feel they've exhausted all treatment options, that's when we should be having a far better culture of clinical research, so that patients through their clinical research participation often feel that they are given hope when they have run out of therapeutic options. . . . [W]e should be all focusing on Australia being the country to do research, because that is the most compassionate and hope-giving mechanism we can, to get our patients fastest access to these high-cost drugs.

Negotiating More Affordable Prices Some participants emphasized the need for governments to address high drug prices, as the prices of many new therapies put them out of reach of most Australian patients. Participants emphasized the need for payers (in this case, government) to negotiate prices that are affordable for the healthcare system as a whole, even if this means there is a delay in access:

> I think it's reasonable that they can delay to negotiate. . . . I think in terms of the greater benefit of the community and the process and the integrity of their system, they need to be working at some kind of—the issue is that the companies will often come to the table, and so if they gave in too easily. You certainly can't trust the marketplace to decide, that's been shown as a failed economic model for the world.

Increased transparency by pharmaceutical companies around how drug prices are set, increased government support for early phase studies to reduce pharmaceutical company research and development costs, and reducing the period of patent exclusivity were also identified as possible solutions. However, participants acknowledged the difficulty of government taking action on drug prices, given the small size of the Australian market and the role that overseas parent companies (particularly those in the United States) play in setting drug prices.

Enrolling Patients in Industry Compassionate Access Schemes Participants expressed different views on the usefulness of industry compassionate access schemes. Some noted positive experiences with these programmes to gain access to medicines for their patients, sometimes for long periods of time. However, others noted limitations such as the commercial risk that these programmes present to industry, the pressure that they place on funders to provide subsidy for these medicines even if the data are equivocal, uncertainty surrounding a patient's ability to access a drug through these programmes (as not all indications may be covered and the programme could be closed at any time), and lost opportunities for data collection if patients receive access through these programmes rather than by participating in a clinical trial:

> [If] we use their so-called compassionate access schemes, we subvert what we really want to do, which is enrol patients on clinical trials. Every patient that is not treated on a clinical trial is an opportunity lost. The data is lost, and it's dreadful.

Supporting Managed Entry Schemes   Some participants advocated for the use of managed entry and coverage with evidence development schemes. Here, subsidy is provided for a medicine at a price justified by the evidence available at the time a decision is made, on the condition that further data are collected to confirm its safety, efficacy, and/or cost-effectiveness in order to determine ongoing subsidy and the final price paid. Some participants commended the ability of these schemes to share risk among all stakeholders. However, others criticized them for being almost entirely in the interests of pharmaceutical companies, as they allow companies to make a profit on drugs that later prove to be unsafe or ineffective:

> Well I don't think [these schemes are] in the public, general public interest, they're in the drug company's interest, because not only do they get their money back sooner, they make a profit on a drug that might not actually work, which is pretty impressive.

Implementing Special Funds   Finally, some participants saw a role for special funds to provide immediate access to medicines that are not subsidized by payers for specified diseases, particularly in the period between registration and provision of subsidy. However, others thought that it would be difficult to restrict this to a few diseases and this approach would quickly become unsustainable:

> And again what you were saying earlier about the slippery slope is that we can take one of those groups and say, OK, well if we're going to add an individual funding or a separate funding mechanism for cancer drugs and then run the risk of upsetting the dementia community, or the whatever community, the rare immunological disease community. So again, where do you draw the line?

Discussion

This study provides new insights into the conflicting demands on physicians and the ways in which they navigate the tensions between their duties to provide patients with hope and compassionate care on the one hand and their duties to protect patients and health systems on the other hand. Physicians emphasized the potential difficulty of navigating these tensions and discussed strategies that they have used with varying degrees of success to achieve this (including preventing cognitive dissonance by disaggregating roles and deferring to experts and policymakers, understanding and managing their own cognitive dissonance, and finding alternative ways for patients to gain access to high-cost medicines). Importantly, disaggregating roles or deferring to "higher" decision-making bodies or processes was possible only—at least ethically—where these bodies and systems were perceived to be fair, rigorous, and impartial.

These types of strategies have been described by others who have noted the competing roles and responsibilities that physicians have within complex healthcare systems when they are expected to serve the interests of both the individual patient and the broader community. Holm (2011), for example, has argued that when engaged in direct patient care, it is acceptable for physicians to "forget" that they are a taxpayer, someone who works for a government department or advisory body, or a member of society and to act purely in the interests of the patient in front of them (i.e. for physicians to exercise partiality). In this case, it is appropriate to reassure physicians that the interests of the broader healthcare system can still be served if they privilege the interests of their individual patients in this way. Along similar lines, Tilburt (2014) has advocated for the need for greater specificity about what is required for physicians to fulfil their potentially competing duties. He argues that priority should be assigned between different commitments and for specification of how different duties are to be fulfilled in different situations. He also advocates for a need to define different spheres where different duties take precedence—for example, in the patient care setting the needs of each individual patient are paramount, whereas other considerations such as appropriate stewardship of resources take priority when physicians are acting in a health policy role (such as a member of a health technology assessment committee); this approach is termed "role morality" (Applbaum 1999).

Alternatively, dissonance could be reduced—or at least normalized—by reassuring doctors that there are a number of possible correct actions when we have greater healthcare needs than our resources can support and that what is right for the patient in front of them will not necessarily also be the right thing for the broader community (and vice versa). Physicians could also be reminded that we live in a liberal democratic society, where individuals hold diverse views which may all be equally valid (this is termed "moral pluralism" or "value pluralism"). Other ways in which dissonance could be reduced include increasing physician understanding and knowledge of health technology assessment and resource allocation processes to make it easier for them to see the "big picture" and defer to restrictions placed by administrators, strengthening resource allocation processes so that it is easier for physicians to focus on advocating for the interests of their patients without fear of undermining these processes to the public detriment, and raising awareness of alternative pathways for accessing medicines to help satisfy physicians that their patients can get access to most medicines when they really need it.

Conclusion

This chapter adds to a growing literature on the tension between a physician's role as a provider of hope and compassionate care on the one hand and as a protector of patients and health systems on the other. We have generated a detailed understanding of how physicians experience and navigate these tensions in the context of prescribing high-cost cancer medicines in Australia. This is an important area of study, as physicians are likely to be faced with these tensions for as long as we have limited healthcare resources and there is a need to prioritize the most effective treatments for funding. Although these tensions are unlikely to ever be fully resolved, there are several practical steps that can be taken to assist those physicians who struggle with cognitive dissonance.

References

ABIM Foundation, ACP-ASIM Foundation, and European Federation of Internal Medicine. 2002. Medical professionalism in the new millennium: A physician charter. *Annals of Internal Medicine* 136(3): 243–246.

Accelerated access review: Final report. 2017. London: Crown Copyright.

Applbaum, A.I. 1999. *Ethics for adversaries: The morality of roles in public and professional life.* Princeton, NJ: Princeton University Press.

Australian Medical Association. 2016. *AMA code of ethics 2004. Editorially revised 2006. Revised 2016.* Canberra: Australian Medical Association. https://ama.com. au/sites/default/files/documents/AMA%20Code%20of%20Ethics%202004.%20 Editorially%20Revised%202006.%20Revised%202016_0.pdf. Accessed January 25, 2018.

Australian Senate Community Affairs Reference Committee. 2015. *Availability of new, innovative and specialist cancer drugs in Australia.* Canberra: Commonwealth of Australia.

Bach, P.B., S.A. Giralt, and L.B. Saltz. 2017. FDA approval of Tisagenlecleucel: Promise and complexities of a $475000 cancer drug. *JAMA* 318(19): 1861–1862.

Banzi, R., C. Gerardi, V. Bertele, and S. Garattini. 2015. Approvals of drugs with uncertain benefit-risk profiles in Europe. *European Journal of Internal Medicine* 26(8): 572–584.

Cancer Drugs Alliance. 2018. *Demand access to timely and affordable medicines.* Sydney: Cancer Drugs Alliance. www.cancerdrugsalliance.org.au. Accessed January 25, 2018.

Cashin, C., Y.-L. Chi, P. Smith, M. Borowitz, and S. Thomson. 2014. *Paying for performance in health care: Implications for health system performance and accountability.* New York, NY: WHO.

Centers for Disease Control and Prevention. 2017. *Health expenditures.* U.S. Department of Health and Human Services. www.cdc.gov/nchs/fastats/health-expenditures. htm. Accessed January 25, 2018.

Charmaz, K. 2006. *Constructing grounded theory: A practical guide through qualitative analysis.* London: Sage Publications.

Chee, T.T., A.M. Ryan, J.H. Wasfy, and W.B. Borden. 2016. Current state of value-based purchasing programs. *Circulation* 133(22): 2197–2205.

Crowe, K. 2017. Alexion Pharmaceuticals ordered to lower price of Soliris in Canada. *CBC News*, September 27. www.cbc.ca/news/health/solaris-pmprb-1.4310249. Accessed January 25, 2018.

Davis, C., H. Naci, E. Gurpinar, E. Poplavska, A. Pinto, and A. Aggarwal. 2017. Availability of evidence of benefits on overall survival and quality of life of cancer drugs approved by European Medicines Agency: Retrospective cohort study of drug approvals 2009–13. *British Medical Journal* 359: j4530.

Department of Health. 2018. *Pharmaceutical benefits fees, patient contributions and safety net thresholds*. Canberra: Commonwealth of Australia. www.pbs.gov.au/info/healthpro/explanatory-notes/front/fee. Accessed January 25, 2018.

Dore, G., and M. Martinello. 2016. Weekly dose: Sofosbuvir: What's the price of a hepatitis C cure? *The Conversation*, August 3. https://theconversation.com/weekly-dose-sofosbuvir-whats-the-price-of-a-hepatitis-c-cure-63208. Accessed January 25, 2018.

Edwards, B. 2016. Cancer drugs: The case for Keytruda. *NBR*, March 3. www.nbr.co.nz/opinion/nz-politics-daily-cancer-drugs-case-keytruda. Accessed January 25, 2018.

Fojo, T., S. Mailankody, and A. Lo. 2014. Unintended consequences of expensive cancer therapeutics: The pursuit of marginal indications and a me-too mentality that stifles innovation and creativity: The John Conley lecture. *JAMA Otolaryngol—Head and Neck Surgery* 140(12): 1225–1236.

Gallagher, S., and M. Little. 2017. Doctors on values and advocacy: A qualitative and evaluative study. *Health Care Analysis* 25(4): 370–385.

Gallego, G., S.J. Taylor, and J.-A. Brien. 2007. Provision of pharmaceuticals in Australian hospitals: Equity of access? *Pharmacy World and Science* 29(2): 47–50.

Ghinea, N., W. Lipworth, R. Day, A. Hill, D.J. Dore, and M. Danta. 2017. Importation of generic hepatitis C therapies: Bridging the gap between price and access in high-income countries. *Lancet* 389(10075): 1268–1272.

Ghinea, N., W. Lipworth, and M. Little. 2017. Access to high cost cancer medicines through the lens of an Australian senate inquiry: Defining the "goods" at stake. *Journal of Bioethical Inquiry* 14(3): 401–410.

Goldhill, O. 2015. 25,450 Americans will die this year waiting for cancer drugs that could treat them. *Quartz*, November 22. https://qz.com/556638/25450-americans-will-die-this-year-waiting-for-cancer-drugs-that-could-treat-them/. Accessed January 25, 2018.

Health Services Research Association of Australia and New Zealand. 2016. *Health expenditure Australia 2014–15*. Canberra: Health Services Research Association Australia and New Zealand, October 6. www.hsraanz.org/health-expenditure-australia-2014-15/. Accessed January 25, 2018.

Hirschler, B. 2016. Biden vows to expedite approval of cancer therapies. *Huffington Post*, January 20. www.huffingtonpost.com/entry/biden-pledges-faster-us-approval-for-cancer-drug-cocktails_us_569fb82fe4b0875553c28338. Accessed January 25, 2018.

Holm, S. 2011. Can "giving preference to my patients" be explained as a role related duty in public health care systems? *Health Care Analysis* 19(1): 89–97.

Huddle, T.S. 2005. Viewpoint: Teaching professionalism: Is medical morality a competency? *Academic Medicine* 80(10): 885–891.

———. 2011. Perspective: Medical professionalism and medical education should not involve commitments to political advocacy. *Academic Medicine* 86(3): 378.

———. 2013. The limits of social justice as an aspect of medical professionalism. *Journal of Medicine and Philosophy* 38(4): 369–387.

———. 2014. Political activism is not mandated by medical professionalism. *American Journal of Bioethics* 14(9): 51–53.

Joffe, S., and H.F. Lynch. 2018. Federal right-to-try legislation: Threatening the FDA's public health mission. *New England Journal of Medicine* 378(8): 695–697.

Jordens, C.F.C. 2000. Outcome studies: An ethical perspective. In *Surgery, ethics and the law*, edited by B. Dooley, M. Fearnside, and M. Gorton, 63–73. Melbourne: Blackwell Science Asia.

Kaplan, S. 2017. Who you calling "slow"? FDA may bristle at Trump's latest dig. *STAT News*, March 1. www.statnews.com/2017/03/01/fda-trump-approval-process/. Accessed January 25, 2018.

Kim, C., and V. Prasad. 2015. Cancer drugs approved on the basis of a surrogate end point and subsequent overall survival: An analysis of 5 years of US Food and Drug Administration approvals. *JAMA Internal Medicine* 175(12): 1992–1994.

Kopelman, L.M. 1999. Help from Hume reconciling professionalism and managed care. *Journal of Medicine and Philosophy* 24(4): 396–410.

Light, D.W., and D. Hughes. 2001. Introduction: A sociological perspective on rationing: Power, rhetoric and situated practices. *Sociology of Health & Illness* 23(5): 551–569.

Medical Board of Australia. 2014. *Good medical practice: A code of conduct for doctors in Australia*. Melbourne: Medical Board of Australia. www.medicalboard.gov.au/Codes-Guidelines-Policies/Code-of-conduct.aspx. Accessed January 25, 2018.

Montgomery, K., and E.S. Schneller. 2007. Hospitals' strategies for orchestrating selection of physician preference items. *Milbank Quarterly* 85(2): 307–335.

Morse, J.M. 1994. "Emerging from the data": The cognitive processes of analysis in qualitative inquiry. In *Critical issues in qualitative research methods*, edited by J.M. Morse, 23–43. Thousand Oaks, CA: Sage Publications.

OECD. 2016. *Health at a glance: Europe 2016—State of health in the EU cycle*. Paris: OECD Publishing.

———. 2017. *Pharmaceutical spending*. Geneva: OECD Publishing. https://data.oecd.org/healthres/pharmaceutical-spending.htm. Accessed January 25, 2018.

Pace, J., S.-A. Pearson, and W. Lipworth. 2015. Improving the legitimacy of medicines funding decisions: A critical literature review. *Therapeutic Innovation and Regulatory Science* 49(3): 364–368.

Paige, L. 2015. Value-based payments: But is there any value for doctors? *Medscape*, October 8. www.medscape.com/viewarticle/848306. Accessed January 25, 2018.

Pellegrino, E.D. 1986. Rationing health care: The ethics of medical gatekeeping. *Journal of Contemporary Health Law and Policy* 2: 23–45.

Pray, L.A. 2008. Gleevec: The breakthrough in cancer treatment. *Nature Education* 1(1): 37.

Rupp, T., and D. Zuckerman. 2017. Quality of life, overall survival, and costs of cancer drugs approved based on surrogate endpoints. *JAMA Internal Medicine* 177(2): 276–277.

Sansom, L., W. Delaat, and J. Horvath. 2015. *Review of medicines and medical devices regulation: Report on the regulatory framework for medicines and medical devices*. Canberra: Australian Government Department of Health.

Tilburt, J.C. 2014. Addressing dual agency: Getting specific about the expectations of professionalism. *American Journal of Bioethics* 14(9): 29–36.

Veatch, R.M. 1990. Physicians and cost containment: The ethical conflict. *Jurimetrics* 30(4): 461–482.

———. 2009. The sources of professional ethics: Why professions fail. *The Lancet* 373(9668): 1000–1001.

———. 2012. Hippocratic, religious, and secular ethics: The points of conflict. *Theoretical Medicine and Bioethics* 33(1): 33–43.

5 Managing and Regulating Conflicts of Interest in Medicine

Wendy Lipworth and Kathleen Montgomery

Background

The medical profession has long been considered an elite group. This high esteem stems from the essential role its members are perceived to play in helping to preserve the health and well-being of their communities, and the advanced level of education and expertise necessary to carry out their obligations. As such, members of the medical profession are given substantial autonomy to conduct their clinical and research work and are allowed to determine for themselves how they will be trained, credentialed, monitored, and reimbursed for their services (Friedson 1970). In return, there is the expectation that they will be committed to their patients, research participants, or the general public and not concerned primarily with their own financial enrichment (Miller 2009; Scott 2014). Any evidence of financial greed on their part is viewed as a kind of betrayal of a social contract (Dean 2015; Taitsman 2011; DeAngelis 2017).

At the same time, it is a reality in today's healthcare environment that medical professionals engage in a variety of ways with commercial entities, in particular the companies that produce and market pharmaceuticals and medical devices (henceforth, health-related industries). In some cases, clinicians become employees or representatives of these industries, often as senior managers overseeing clinical research, regulatory, and health economic processes. For many other health professionals, the relationship with health-related industries is more subtle and indirect. For example, a large proportion of doctors' continuing medical education is now funded by the pharmaceutical industry (Steinbrook 2011; Steinman, Landefeld, and Baron 2012), and the pharmaceutical industry also funds the vast majority of large clinical trials (Califf et al. 2012). Medical professionals also frequently engage with health-related industries as key opinion leaders, who both consult to companies and educate other medical professionals about these companies' products (Steensma 2015).

The relationships between medical professionals and health-related industries are highly controversial, both because of the way that information is presented to medical professionals and because of the conflicts of interest that relationships with industry can create. The concern here is that the more medical professionals rely on industry, the more committed they become to the "hands that feed" them (Angell 2004; Avorn 2005; Elliott 2010; Healy 2012; DeAngelis 2017). While loyalty to industry and commercial self-interest are not in themselves immoral, they have the potential to create situations in which commitments to industry, or to the self, become privileged over commitments to patients, research participants, and the public.

Those with concerns about industry-related conflict of interest (henceforth, COI) use a number of strategies to convince people of the dangers that lurk beneath the surface of all relationships between medical professionals and health-related industries. They tell compelling causal stories, linking COI to both individual and institutional corruption (Rodwin 2012); they generate and cite evidence that COIs lead medical professionals to behave in morally questionable and potentially harmful ways (Lundh et al. 2012); they emphasize the psychological inevitability that those who interact with industry will be affected by these interactions, citing theories of unconscious reasoning and decision-making and the persuasive power of the gift relationship (Dana and Loewenstein 2003); and they tell distressing stories about "real-world" harms to patients, research participants, and health systems that seem to be causally linked to COI on the part of medical professionals (Davies 2013). With these concerns in mind, critics of industry interactions call for measures such as disclosure, transparency, punishment, and proscription of certain kinds of industry interactions (Institute of Medicine 2009).

The "COI movement," as it is sometimes called, has had wide-ranging effects on health and medicine. Many major hospitals, medical schools, research institutes, academic journals, and policy organizations now have conflict of interest policies. These policies might proscribe certain activities (e.g. doctors receiving large gifts from industry or people with conflicts of interest writing review articles for medical journals). Alternatively, an activity might be allowed but need to be disclosed.

Although the COI movement has gained significant traction internationally, there is a small but increasingly vocal counter-discourse that questions the negative attention focused on relationships between medical professionals and health-related industries. Participants in this counter-discourse argue that it is impossible to prove that COI results in harm to patients, research participants, and health systems. They also challenge the idea that industry interactions are a cause of institutional or professional corruption, seeing them instead as a feature of modern medicine that can be both beneficial and easily managed through conscious moral reflection (Barton, Stossel, and Stell 2014; Shaywitz and Stossel 2009; Stell 2010; Stossel and Stell 2011).

Debates about COI in healthcare have become quite hostile, with claims that those who interact with industry are corrupt or "for sale" (Angell 2009; Rodwin 2012). In return, those with concerns about COI are referred to as, among other things, members of an ideological movement or as "pharmascolds" engaging in character assassination of those with so-called conflicts of interest (Barton, Stossel, and Stell 2014; Shaywitz and Stossel 2009; Stell 2010).

While the literature on the pharmaceutical industry is polarized between strong critics and strong defenders of industry interactions, practitioners themselves express a greater degree of uncertainty. In a qualitative interview study of Australian medical specialists, for example, Doran et al. (2006) found that clinicians could be categorized into three groups: those who engage confidently with industry, those who avoid industry altogether, and those who engage, but do so with ambivalence, because they recognize both the risks and benefits of industry interaction. In a more recent qualitative study of medical professionals' attitudes towards industry influence and COI, Williams et al. (2017) found a wide variety of perspectives regarding the causes of COIs, their moral significance, and how they should be managed. Other studies have revealed similar heterogeneity and ambivalence on the part of clinicians, researchers, and policymakers about the pharmaceutical industry and the ways in which medical professionals engage with it (Prosser, Almond, and Walley 2003; Glaser and Bero 2005).

Organizations, including universities, teaching hospitals, and governments also display considerable heterogeneity in their approach to COI, with some setting strict rules regarding industry influence and conflict of interest and others being far more lenient. For example, the American Medical Student Association (AMSA) rated United States medical schools' conflict of interest policies and found enormous variation in the existence and enforcement of COI policies (American Medical Student Association 2016). Even in biomedical publishing, where it is now the norm to request disclosure of authors' conflicts of interest, such policies are applied and enforced inconsistently (Dunn et al. 2016). Organization-level ambivalence about the pharmaceutical industry is also evident in the tendency for research organizations to demand that biomedical researchers engage with industry and commercialize their discoveries while also demanding that such practices be limited, disclosed, and defended (Zinner et al. 2010; Chapman et al. 2012). In the medical policymaking setting, ambivalence emerges when committees are simultaneously expected to include members with relevant expertise—which often includes people with close ties to industry—and to ensure that such committees are independent (Rockey and Collins 2010; Norris et al. 2012).

There is, therefore, an obvious quandary at the heart of medical practice regarding the appropriate ways of managing interactions between medical professions and health-related industries. To date, little empirical research has been conducted that focuses on how medical professionals think industry interactions and COI should be managed. In what follows, we present the results of two empirical studies that explore this issue. We turn first to a published debate surrounding medical professionals' involvement with the pharmaceutical industry. We then present data from interviews with medical professionals who are employed within the pharmaceutical industry.

Study One: The Rosenbaum Debate

In May 2015, the *New England Journal of Medicine* published a series of articles by Lisa Rosenbaum (Rosenbaum 2015a, 2015b, 2015c)—a National Correspondent for the journal and also a Harvard cardiologist. In these articles, Rosenbaum called for a softening of attitudes towards medical professionals who interact with the pharmaceutical industry. Her articles were accompanied by an editorial by Jeffrey Drazen (Editor-in-Chief of the journal since 2000), in which he hinted that the *New England Journal of Medicine* might do away with its requirement that authors of review and educational articles should not have ties to industry (Drazen 2015).

The Rosenbaum articles and Drazen editorial generated a firestorm of criticism in both the biomedical literature and in health-related blogs. The major backlash occurred in the pages of the *British Medical Journal (BMJ)*. Critical editorials were penned by Fiona Godlee (current Editor-in-Chief of the *BMJ*, who has written extensively about publication ethics), Elizabeth Loder (a clinical editor at the *BMJ*), and Catherine Brizzell (head of education at the *BMJ*) (Godlee 2015; Loder, Brizzell, and Godlee 2015). The *BMJ* also published a critical essay by Robert Steinbrook, Jerome Kassirer, and Marcia Angell, all of whom have held senior editorial roles at major medical journals, and have been instrumental in establishing conflict of interest policies (Steinbrook, Kassirer, and Angell 2015). Other criticisms were evident in a news article (McCarthy 2015) and a letter (Lenzer and Brownlee 2015) published in the *BMJ* and in more than thirty health-related blogs. More supportive editorials were written by the editors of the *Annals of Internal Medicine* (The Editors 2015) and by Richard Horton, Editor-in-Chief of *The Lancet* (Horton 2015). Numerous informal responses were also published online, mostly in the form of blogs, the majority of which were highly critical of Rosenbaum's position.

Method

In order to critically analyze the above debate (henceforth, the Rosenbaum debate), we identified the relevant responses using a variety of search terms (e.g. "Rosenbaum," "Drazen," and "conflict of interest" or "pharmaceutical industry") in general databases including Web of Science and Google Scholar and by following references within sources to other sources. We then analyzed these materials qualitatively, drawing on both Morse's outline of the cognitive basis of qualitative research (1994) and Charmaz's outline of data analysis in grounded theory (2006). This procedure involves initial line-by-line coding, synthesis of codes into categories, focused coding using these categories, and abstracting into analytic categories. A coding tree was generated. Throughout the data analysis, a process of constant comparison was employed. Existing codes and analytic categories were refined, enriched, and reorganized as new codes and categories were developed or as similarities and differences were recognized. Enough material was analyzed to ensure that categories were saturated and all analytic categories were fully described and well understood. Thematic saturation was reached after approximately half the material had been analyzed. In what follows, we present the views of participants on both sides of the debate regarding the appropriate management of industry interactions and industry-related conflict of interest.

Results

Point of Agreement: Industry Interactions Are Important but Need to Be Controlled

Rosenbaum and her critics disagreed profoundly about the extent and nature of harms associated with interactions between medical professionals and health-related industries, with Rosenbaum seeing industry interactions as being largely beneficial and her critics seeing them as serious threats to patient well-being and public trust. Nonetheless, both Rosenbaum and her critics agreed on the need for some degree of regulation of industry interactions. Rosenbaum acknowledged that such interactions need to be known and accounted for and that some checks and balances are needed. For example, she spoke approvingly of committees that put firewalls in place to avoid undue influence from members who have ties to industry. She also admitted that some kinds of industry interactions, such as "securing physicians' loyalty with Hawaiian vacations" should be prohibited. For her, the key question was:

> [H]ow to best manage conflicts of interest while preserving the collaborations on which medical advances depend.
>
> (Rosenbaum 2015a, 1861)

While Rosenbaum's critics emphasized how harmful interactions with industry can be, they too acknowledged that academic collaboration is necessary to move medical science forward as long as this is limited and carefully controlled:

> Unmistakably, collaborations between academia and industry can speed medical progress and benefit patients. Such partnerships, however, can flourish with far less money in aggregate flowing from drug and device manufacturers to physicians and their institutions, and without the web of other lucrative ties between industry and physicians that lack a clear scientific or medical purpose.
>
> (Steinbrook, Kassirer, and Angell 2015, ¶3 under "Straw men")

Point of Contention: Individual-Level Regulation Versus Profession-Level Regulation

Although both Rosenbaum and her critics argued for some degree of regulation of industry interactions, there was a strong difference between the two sides in terms of whether they thought that the responsibility for such regulation should reside primarily in the hands of individual physicians (individual-level regulation) or in the hands of the profession as a whole (profession-level regulation) through generalized and proscriptive policies and procedures.

Rosenbaum argued for individual-level regulation of industry interactions, emphasizing both the weaknesses in professional-level regulation and the effectiveness of individual-level regulation. Her critics refuted each of her arguments, instead making the case for profession-level regulation.

PROFESSION-LEVEL REGULATION IS NOT EVIDENCE BASED

Rosenbaum argued at length that current profession-level approaches to regulation of industry interactions and COI have not been driven and shaped by evidence of either a need for them or their effectiveness in improving patient outcomes:

> Although everyone agrees that patients' health should not be compromised by physicians' desire for financial gain, the extent to which physicians' primary and secondary interests actually conflict, under what circumstances, and at what cost are unknown.
>
> (Rosenbaum 2015c, 1959)

Rather, she maintained, profession-level regulations have been driven and shaped by anti-industry emotions, intuitions, and cognitive biases triggered by a series of scandals:

> Conflict-of-interest policies have evolved not through careful data gathering and analysis but through intensification of regulations after each big scandal.
>
> (Rosenbaum 2015a, 2065)

Critics of Rosenbaum, in contrast, forcefully denied that there is a lack of evidence of harm stemming from industry influence and conflict of interest, arguing that:

> Pharmaceutical company money, and the purchase of influence, has been the single most powerful distorting force in healthcare in a generation—this is undisputed.
>
> (Stone 2015, ¶5)

They argued that, while perhaps not evidence based in the sense of being underpinned by randomized trials, profession-level policies are a necessary precaution in the face of obvious risk:

> One thing here is true—no, we don't have prospective randomized trials showing that conflict of interest policies improve patient outcomes. But, such a stance is absurd.
>
> (Prasad 2015, ¶6)

In this way, they justified the need for profession-level proscription of particular kinds of activities:

> Physicians who develop products and hold patents or receive royalties should not evaluate the product. Other types of payments, such as speakers' and other personal fees, payments to be ghost authors of review articles, and ill-defined consulting arrangements, distort physicians' work and undermine our independence, as has been repeatedly documented. And there are no excuses for outright gifts, such as meals, travel, lodging expenses, and entertainment.
>
> (Steinbrook, Kassirer, and Angell 2015, ¶3 under "Straw men")

Some went even further, arguing for the need to "push back against the capitalization and invasion of medicine by industry" (1 Boring Old Man 2015, final paragraph) through "culture change . . . in the interests of patients and the public" (Godlee 2015, ¶7) and for the need to "improve the incentive structure such that the goal of maximizing human health remains paramount" (Prasad 2015, ¶19 under "Conclusion").

PROFESSION-LEVEL REGULATION CAN BE COUNTERPRODUCTIVE

According to Rosenbaum, profession-level control of physician behaviour is not only based on limited evidence but also has a number of adverse consequences. The most obvious of these is a loss of what she perceives to be necessary relationships with industry. She warned us:

> Perhaps effective therapies are adopted more slowly when industry representatives are banned from our workplace. Perhaps we miss opportunities to understand complex medical topics because experts aren't permitted to write about them. Perhaps life-saving therapies whose development requires the combined talents of clinicians and industry scientists don't materialize.
>
> (Rosenbaum 2015a, 2068)

Another adverse consequence of profession-level regulation, according to Rosenbaum, is a paradoxical loss of trust in science and medicine. According to this view, trust is impaired not by industry interactions and conflict of interest themselves but by the "spiral of blame and shame" triggered by the "conflict-of-interest movement." She described the dynamic as follows:

> As reputational costs of exposure grow, everyone works harder at damage control, and fewer people defend themselves, because self-justifications may only intensify the criticism; those who are exposed just hope it will go away quietly. As the public observes this spiral of blame and shame, the conflict-of-interest movement has paradoxically achieved what it set out to avert: an erosion of public trust in medicine and science.
>
> (Rosenbaum 2015a, 2067)

Critics of Rosenbaum challenged the idea that profession-level conflict of interest policies have done more harm than good. They claimed that Rosenbaum's arguments about the "purported harms of conflict of interest policies and regulations" are "fanciful and data-free" (Steinbrook, Kassirer, and Angell 2015, ¶1 under "Straw men"), arguing:

> Rosenbaum claims that limiting conflicts of interest will kill the golden goose of medical innovation. Really? Does that mean the academic researchers who do not have conflicts of interest have nothing to offer the world in the way of cures?
>
> (Brownlee 2015, ¶7 under "He who pays the piper calls the tune")

Her critics also challenged Rosenbaum's claim that the main threat to trust in medicine is profession-level "blame and shame." For them, it is reliance on industry and the conflicts stemming from this reliance, that erode trust. As one blogger put it:

> I and many others suggest that the "stories about industry greed" have not permeated enough, and that this problem has polluted much of medical research and medical practice, to the point where trust of the medical research enterprise has been eroded.
>
> (Molchan 2015, ¶3)

THE EFFECTIVENESS OF INDIVIDUAL-LEVEL REGULATION IS UNDERESTIMATED

In addition to arguing that profession-level regulation is unsophisticated and counterproductive, Rosenbaum argued that it is *unnecessary* because individual clinicians are trustworthy and capable of detecting and managing their own conflicts of interest. She wrote at length about the failure of the profession as a whole to acknowledge this trustworthiness, bemoaning the "loud chorus of shaming" that afflicts medical professionals who interact with industry and the tendency of critics to generalize, such that "the bad behaviour of the few has facilitated impugning of the many." In an effort to put forward a less negative view of individual physicians who interact with industry, Rosenbaum called for a more sophisticated understanding of bias and conflict of interest in medicine. First, she argued that a risk of bias is not proof that bias exists, noting:

> Although, by definition, a conflict of interest represents a risk that judgment will be compromised—not a determination that such a lapse has actually occurred—the pharmascolds' narrative about conflicts of interest often conflates the two.
>
> (Rosenbaum 2015c, 1960)

Second, she emphasized that bias is not the same thing as corruption, and observed:

> As the gap between evidence and impressions grows, reasoned approaches to managing financial conflicts are eclipsed by cries of corruption even when none exists.
>
> (Rosenbaum 2015b, 1864)

Following on from these distinctions, she argued that well-motivated medical professionals are able to manage any biases they might have and make decisions that are not only objective but also sometimes contrary to the desires of industry.

In contrast, many of Rosenbaum's critics stressed the importance of being alert to the realities of human nature, where bias is insidious and often unconscious, and to which "none of us is immune":

> Judges are expected to recuse themselves from hearing a case in which there are concerns that they could benefit financially from the outcome. Journalists are expected not to write stories on topics in which they have a financial conflict of interest. The problem, obviously, is that their objectivity might be compromised, either consciously or unconsciously, and there would be no easy way to know whether it had been.
>
> (Steinbrook, Kassirer, and Angell 2015, ¶4)

Furthermore, while Rosenbaum's critics acknowledged that "COIs are not necessarily evil, and people with COIs include many brilliant researchers and clinicians" (Farkas 2015, ¶1 under "Conclusions"), they also insisted that some people are indeed motivated by greed or other personal biases and that their efforts to justify their action are, in some cases, simply attempts "to make a virtue of self-interest" (Steinbrook, Kassirer, and Angell 2015, ¶7 under "Straw men").

The foregoing discussion reflects the positions taken by members of the medical profession regarding the appropriate regulation of industry influence and associated conflict of interest. In essence, Rosenbaum and her supporters argue that profession-level regulation has gone too far and that the effectiveness of individual-level regulation has been underestimated. In the following study, we provide data from individuals who occupy the dual roles of members of the medical profession and employees of health-related industries. We chose to explore this group's views because they face a similar dilemma—how to balance the interests of patients against commercial imperatives, but they occupy a different position in the healthcare organizational field. They may well, therefore, have perspectives on regulation of conflict of interest that differ in instructive ways from those of practicing medical professionals.

Study Two: Professionals Working for Health-Related Industries

Method

We conducted fifteen face-to-face interviews with health professionals working in the medical and drug development departments of nine pharmaceutical companies in Sydney, Australia. Our participants represented most of the major companies that have an Australian presence as well as one manufacturer of generic medicines. We used a purposive sampling procedure that allowed us to include participants from as many drug companies as possible. Interviewees were identified first through organizational websites and the professional contacts of the research team and then via snowball sampling from the initial group.

We conducted semi-structured interviews, lasting approximately one and a half hours each. Among the questions were those asking participants to reflect and offer their opinions on issues surrounding drug development and relationships between industry and their practice as professionals. Our procedures for analysis of the qualitative data mirrored those described in Study One. (For additional information about the sample and research methods, see Lipworth, Montgomery, and Little 2013).

Results

In contrast to the Rosenbaum debate, where there was profound disagreement about the compatibility of the goals of industry and those of medical professionals, participants in this study all thought that industry goals and public health goals were largely compatible:

> I liked the philosophy of the company in terms of being very open . . . and putting always the patient first. . . . So patient's health, ensuring that's at the forefront but finding the sweet spot where you can make a buck and do it ethically with the patient at the forefront. I like that approach. . . . I think as you become more and more senior in the medical practice, you start realizing that actually we're both here for the same

purpose, doctors are in it to make a buck, pharmacy companies are in it to make a buck, and they both ultimately succeed when patients' health is improved.

They did not, however, deny that there are differences between commercial entities and those that are oriented solely towards public well-being:

> At the end of the day, we're not a philanthropic organization. And I'm quite happy to say that. I know my part of it and how those drugs were going to get on the market, and that's going to be beneficial, but they do cost money. . . . And then do we make a profit? Yes, we do, we're a business.

They described several ways of regulating the kinds of tensions that arise in this context, which spanned four levels: government, industry, organization, and individual.

Government-Level Regulation

Participants generally spoke positively about government regulation—most commonly with reference to the Australian medicines regulator—the Therapeutic Goods Administration (TGA), which ensures, among other things, that industry does not market its products deceptively or prematurely. The reality of working in a commercial environment, in which some companies will inevitably push the boundaries, was acknowledged:

> We . . . need to be monitored. So while there is commercial gain in anything, you need to have a really good monitoring process in place. Individuals, people will be people. Adam Smith is right, so I guess we'd be Wall Street. You need to have constant safeguards, either internally applied or sanctions externally applied, you can't just let go.

Participants were acutely aware that they would be monitored and spoke with pride about their efforts to comply with regulations:

> You've got to really protect against fraud, you've got to really audit. Now we audit ourselves to make sure everything is hunky-dory, and ethics committees and TGAs [Therapeutic Goods Administrations] are now coming up to where they are also in the position to audit people.

They also noted that compliance with regulatory requirements was a means of avoiding rejections and criticism:

> These documents are very, very carefully worded to accurately reflect what the data really mean. And one of the motivations in that is that if

a pharmaceutical company does not do this, then we are truly open to criticism of the worst kind. And we will be criticized. And so it's not just that people are well meaning. There's a little bit of caution that comes in because of the environment in which we work.

Industry-Level Regulation

In Australia, industry-level regulation of the pharmaceutical industry takes the form of codes of conduct developed by Medicines Australia—the national trade association for manufacturers of prescription medicines. Membership of Medicines Australia is voluntary, but companies that are members are expected to adhere to its policies. Our participants spoke freely and positively—even proudly—about such industry-level policies:

> I think [codes of practice] are a good thing. And they're applied. And the reason they're applied and work is because we dob on each other, basically. So it's a small world and it's a bit incestuous. So if a company misbehaved, every other company would know about it within twenty-four hours and would make a complaint.

Compliance with industry standards was portrayed both as a good in itself and as a moral imperative:

> We operated in a highly professional way, our goal, not that we don't now, but our goal was always to be very highly compliant, not only with our legal and our industry standards, but from the moral and ethical point of view.

Organization-Level Regulation

Participants also spoke with pride about their companies' policies regarding patient well-being and the prevention and management of wrongdoing:

> In my company, I think if there was something funny going on, like it was bordering on the illegal . . . there are well-established procedures for whistle-blowing, and again the company goes out of its way to encourage that, so there's no risk of being allowed to be swept under the carpet.

Participants noted that their companies insist on standards similar to those applied to scientific and clinical work and support such standards when they collaborate with academics and clinicians:

> When we collaborate with an institution, we have a [company] code on fireable offenses; we are not allowed to conduct research unless the researchers are free to publish.

Individual-Level Regulation

Participants gave detailed accounts of two related strategies that they use to personally manage any tensions that they experience between commercial and public health goals: (1) maintaining an identity as a medical professional and (2) acting with personal integrity.

MAINTAINING A MEDICAL PROFESSIONAL IDENTITY

Several participants emphasized the importance of preserving their identities as physicians, pharmacists, or medical researchers, thereby seeing themselves, and being seen by others, as having these identities:

> If I couldn't [preserve my identity] as a clinician, I'd leave [the company]. I consider that your primary role as the health professional working in the pharmaceutical industry is as a patient champion, to take the rough edges off the commercial imperative of the company.

For some, this entailed keeping a foot in both worlds, for example, by maintaining clinical, research, or teaching roles:

> I still teach. . . . I've got a 0.4 position at [University]

A related of kind identity work that participants described was distinguishing those in medical roles within companies (e.g. in clinical research and regulatory affairs departments) from those involved in sales and marketing:

> So as a medical person, your responsibility is to make sure the patient is safe and that the company isn't put at risk and the patients aren't put at risk.

ACTING WITH PERSONAL INTEGRITY

Perhaps because participants were not naïve to the reputation of the pharmaceutical industry and to the moral quandaries they might personally experience, they were adamant that they operated with a strong sense of personal ethics and integrity:

> In the role I'm in now, absolutely I can make a call to say "No, that's not appropriate, we can't do that."

Several participants emphasized that they would speak up if they observed wrongdoing and would leave a company if they ever felt that their ethical standards were being compromised:

> I've never really felt compromised, that I've had to lower my standards or back down on my standards. I've never had someone, when I've

given really strong advice not to, do it; no one's overridden that. That's why I've stayed for twenty-three years. If I felt compromised I'd leave.

Discussion

The foregoing results demonstrate both the complexities of professional regulation and the differing attitudes that people have towards various modes of regulation. In the Rosenbaum debate, there were strongly divergent views about the compatibility of commercial and public health goals, and two levels of regulation were invoked: profession-level regulation and individual-level regulation. In the study of industry professionals, there was greater agreement about the compatibility of commercial and public health goals—that is that these are compatible but that tensions may arise that should be managed. Industry professionals also recognized and endorsed a wider set of regulatory interventions and from multiple sources: government, industry, organization, and individual. In what follows, we draw on sociological theory to interpret these observations.

Theoretical Interpretation

In his seminal work on the sociology of the professions, Freidson (1970) focused on the ways in which professions are regulated. Freidson emphasized the central role of self-regulation in his examination of how professional powers and autonomy are justified. He noted that the justification for extensive professional autonomy lay in the claim that only other members of the profession have the knowledge and expertise to effectively monitor and regulate the practice of medicine and those who engage in it.

Since Freidson's day, scholars and practitioners have disagreed about whether Freidson intended professional self-regulation to mean an *individual's* regulation of his or her *own* behaviour or to mean profession-level regulation imposed by the profession as a *collective body* by professional associations, healthcare and educational institutions, and other thought leaders such as academic journal editors.

We see this disagreement played out in the Rosenbaum debate. Rosenbaum and her supporters strongly espoused an individualized version of professional self-regulation, whereby individual professionals can be trusted to monitor their own behaviour and actions using both their own moral compasses and norms inculcated by the profession. Her opponents maintained that individual monitoring and self-regulation are inadequate, in large part because of the insidious ways that COI affect professional judgement. Thus, they argued, it is necessary to impose profession-level forms of regulation through policies, guidelines, and restrictions. In either perspective, regulation continues to be fostered by professionals themselves, consistent with Freidson's theory, but the parties to the debate use different lenses through which such professional self-regulation is envisioned to operate.

Leahey and Montgomery (2011) offer a more complex view of professional regulation, which mirrors the results in the industry study—in which government and organization-level regulation were endorsed along with various forms of professional self-regulation. They argue that while the concepts of autonomy and self-regulation persist as fundamental features of professional work, the nature of professional control has evolved in recent decades. They point out that in contrast to the past where professionals were likely to be self-employed entrepreneurs, typically they now work within an organizational setting—as practitioners in medical groups, hospitals or universities and as employees in health-related industries. Along with this shift, there has been a growth in the number and kinds of bodies with an interest in regulating professional behaviour.

Leahey and Montgomery (2011) find that such shifts have been accompanied by changes in attitudes about the trustworthiness of professionals. For example, they argue that, for many years, professional norms and codes of behaviour were developed and used by professionals themselves, internalized through socialization. The prevailing attitude was that "formal policies were not needed because . . . professional activity was effectively self-regulating" (Steneck 1999, 169). As stories of misconduct and questionable practices by professionals, including COIs, began to emerge, scepticism grew about their trustworthiness, and a new era of regulation was ushered in. This has included more oversight, such as hospital ethics committees and strict publication policies, as well as government restrictions on relationships with industry.

Table 5.1 depicts the levels and sources of regulation that have arisen in response to concerns about waning professional trustworthiness and a corresponding growth in scepticism regarding professionals' capacity to be self-regulating.

As depicted in Table 5.1, a complex set of regulations now exists for professionals, whether acting as practitioners or industry employees. These

Table 5.1 Levels and Sources of Regulation of Professional Behaviour

Level of Regulation	Source of Regulation for Practitioners	Source of Regulation for Employees	Type of Regulatory Relationship
Individual	Self	Self	Personal
Organization	Medical Practice Groups	Pharmaceutical Firms	Direct
	Hospitals	Medical Device Firms	
	Universities		
Profession/ Industry	Professional Societies	Industry Associations	Indirect
	Academic Journals	Trade Publications	
	Accreditation Bodies		
Government	Funding Agencies	Medicines Panels	Distant
	Licensing Boards		

regulations move along a continuum from a personal degree of individual self-regulation, to direct regulation at the organization level, to indirect regulation at the profession or industry level, to distant regulation at the government level. It is interesting to note that profession-generated forms of regulation (individual and collective) are interwoven with forms of regulation that are external to the profession (organization and government).

Not surprisingly, as more layers of regulation are developed and imposed, some observers have argued that the pendulum has swung too far away from self-regulation and that professional behaviour has become stifled. In so doing, professional trustworthiness has become undervalued. Indeed, an over-regulation argument is made by a number of observers across sectors of societies.

In addition to differing in terms of which level(s) of regulation they deemed legitimate, an important distinction between the views of those participating in the Rosenbaum debate and those participating in the industry study was that in the Rosenbaum debate, differing levels of regulation were portrayed as competing—if not conflicting—whereas in the industry study, different levels of regulation were viewed as compatible and even synergistic. At one extreme of the Rosenbaum debate are those who believe that COI policies, formulated and enforced at the profession level (e.g. by universities and academic journals), do not go far enough, observing that a commercial bias can creep into decisions without professionals recognizing it. At the other extreme are those who believe that such profession-level regulations have gone too far and have been imposed without careful thought or evidence of their need. People in this camp believe that strict macro-level policies and prohibitions not only are unnecessary but also can do harm—impairing valuable collaborations with health-industry partners and fostering an atmosphere of distrust of professionals who engage in this manner.

In the industry study, in contrast, the various levels of regulation were not seen to be in tension with each other but rather as components of a larger regulatory system. Indeed, in stark contrast to the polarized views expressed in the Rosenbaum debate, at no point in any of the industry interviews did a participant claim that one level of regulation was superior to another.

One possible explanation for this difference is that while healthcare professionals today face multiple levels of regulation (as shown in Table 5.1), they are able to maintain the illusion of being free to self-regulate at the individual level because more macro levels of regulation (including profession-level regulation) operate relatively behind the scenes. These become visible only during moments of confrontation, such as at the funding or publication stage. It is at this stage that the Rosenbaum debate takes place. For professionals working in industry, however, their day-to-day work is predicated on compliance with multiple levels of regulation. Thus, one could argue that professionals in industry have a more realistic appreciation for how professional regulation operates and how it affects, and facilitates, their role within that environment.

Implications for the Medical Profession

Our two studies offer guidance in how to think about appropriate levels of regulation, by highlighting the importance of historical context. It is important to acknowledge that professional self-regulation has evolved since the days when individual self-regulation of one's own behaviour or, to some extent, collective profession-level self-regulation were considered the only acceptable forms of oversight, as anything else would be considered an unacceptable encroachment on one's professional autonomy. Professional norms were inculcated during education and training and informally reinforced throughout one's career by peers. Nevertheless, some professional misconduct undoubtedly failed to be recognized or thwarted within this loose network of individual and profession-level professional regulation.

Recognizing this weakness in the informal regulatory system, and alarmed by the increasing influence of health-related industries on medical research, policymaking, and practice, many believed that the best response would be to formalize and strengthen existing profession-level regulation (by professional organizations, societies, and academic journals) and to impose additional layers of regulation by government bodies. Others, in contrast, have resisted such moves because of concerns that professionals have become over-regulated.

The Rosenbaum debate reflects this dilemma. Rosenbaum appears to envision a return to the days when individual professionals were able to monitor their own behaviour and to forestall potential COIs through conscious self-reflection. Her critics, motivated by a deep distrust of industry influence, espouse a need to strengthen profession-level barriers in order to prevent industry encroachment into professional behaviour. This impasse, in turn, creates quandaries for professionals, who may continue to doubt how best to engage ethically with industry.

In contrast, industry professionals in our study present a more nuanced approach to regulation. These individuals recognize and endorse multiple levels of regulation, as shown on Table 5.1. Indeed, they maintain that such a framework allows them to work with more, rather than less, confidence that their conduct is ethical. This is a revealing finding, we would argue, because it demonstrates that forms of professional regulation need not be pitted against each other. Rather, the various levels of regulations could be seen as complementary strategies that are *all* needed in order to manage an issue as morally, politically, and organizationally complex as that of industry influence and conflict of interest.

Grundy et al. (2017) have illustrated elsewhere that those working for pharmaceutical companies take for granted the need to disclose and manage their own conflicts of interest—such as those stemming from personal relationships or financial arrangements. While these measures were enforced at the organization level, they were not seen as controversial or punitive but rather simply as part of ethical business practice. It is not entirely clear why the culture that medical professionals inhabit has evolved in such a way that conflicts of interest are viewed as being shameful and efforts to manage them as impositions. It is possible that this attitude has to do with a combination of the ways in which COIs are portrayed by those with concerns about them and medical professionals' self-perception as members of a caring profession who should not ever be susceptible to bias (Chapman, Kaatz, and Carnes 2013). Whatever the reason, medicine could, somewhat ironically, benefit from becoming more like private industry in which conflict of interest is seen as a set of circumstances in need of management, rather than a personal moral failure (Grundy et al. 2017).

Limitations and Future Research

Insights from our study may be valuable for professional practitioners worried about how to think about their own behaviour and the potential for conflict of interest when they interact with industry. However, we caution that the studies are limited to a snapshot of a debate among professionals engaged in a public discussion and a small set of professionals working in industry. Larger studies in other settings would augment, and may modify, the interpretations we report here. In particular, it would be important to gather in-depth data from practicing health professionals regarding what they perceive to be appropriate level(s) of regulation.

Conclusion

Medical professionals have long enjoyed considerable autonomy, both as individuals and as members of a profession that is trusted to set and maintain its own standards. The commercialization of the healthcare organizational field is one of many forces (along with managerialism, consumerism, etc.) that has reduced trust in medical professionals and raised the possibility that profession-level regulations need to be strengthened and external regulations imposed. As the Rosenbaum debate illustrates, such moves are likely to be met with considerable resistance from medical professionals who believe that they can personally manage their industry interactions and associated conflicts of interest. Industry employees' more nuanced attitudes towards both conflict of interest and regulation thereof provide an alternative model from which medical professionals could—somewhat paradoxically—learn.

References

1 Boring Old Man. *A narrative.* . . . *1 Boring Old Man*, May 24. http://1boringoldman. com/index.php/2015/05/24/a-narrative/. Accessed January 23, 2018.

American Medical Student Association. 2016. *AMSA scorecard 2016*. http://amsascore card.org/. Accessed October 28, 2017.

Angell, M. 2004. *The truth about the drug companies: How they deceive us and what to do about it*. New York, NY: Random House Trade Paperbacks.

————. 2009. Drug companies & doctors: A story of corruption. *The New York Review of Books* 56(1): 8–12.

Avorn, J. 2005. *Powerful medicines: The benefits, risks and costs of prescription drugs.* New York, NY: Vintage Books.

Barton, D., T. Stossel, and L. Stell. 2014. After 20 years, industry critics bury skeptics, despite empirical vacuum. *International Journal of Clinical Practice* 68(6): 666–673.

Brownlee, S. 2015. The conflict denialists strike back. *Lown Institute Blog*, May 29. http://lowninstitute.org/news/the-conflict-denialists-strike-back/. Accessed January 23, 2018.

Califf, R., D.A. Zarin, J.M. Kramer, R.E. Sherman, L.H. Aberle, and A. Tasneem. 2012. Characteristics of clinical trials registered in ClinicalTrials.gov, 2007–2010. *JAMA* 307(17): 1838–1847.

Chapman, E.N., A. Kaatz, and M. Carnes. 2013. Physicians and implicit bias: How doctors may unwittingly perpetuate health care disparities. *Journal of General Internal Medicine* 28(11): 1504–1510.

Chapman, S., B. Morrell, R. Forsyth, I. Kerridge, and C. Stewart. 2012. Policies and practices on competing interests of academic staff in Australian universities. *Medical Journal of Australia* 196(7): 452–456.

Charmaz, K. 2006. *Constructing grounded theory: A practical guide through qualitative analysis.* London, Thousand Oaks, CA and New Delhi: Sage Publications.

Dana, J., and G. Loewenstein. 2003. A social science perspective on gifts to physicians from industry. *JAMA* 290(2): 252–255.

Davies, E. 2013. Investigating the fallout of a suicide. *BMJ* 347: f6039.

Dean, J. 2015. Private practice is unethical: And doctors should give it up. *BMJ* 350: h2299.

DeAngelis, C.D. 2017. Medicine: A profession in distress. *The Milbank Quarterly*, November 14, online exclusive. www.milbank.org/quarterly/articles/medicine-profession-distress/

Doran, E., I. Kerridge, P. McNeill, and D. Henry. 2006. Empirical uncertainty and moral contest: A qualitative analysis of the relationship between medical specialists and the pharmaceutical industry in Australia. *Social Science & Medicine* 62(6): 1510–1519.

Drazen, J.M. 2015. Revisiting the commercial: Academic interface. *New England Journal of Medicine* 372(19): 1853–1854.

Dunn, A.G., E. Coiera, K.D. Mandl, and F.T. Bourgeois. 2016. Conflict of interest disclosure in biomedical research: A review of current practices, biases, and the role of public registries in improving transparency. *Research Integrity and Peer Review* 1(1): 1.

The Editors. 2015. Walking the tightrope of academia-industry relationships. *Annals of Internal Medicine* 163(6): 477–478.

Elliott, C. 2010. *White coat, black hat: Adventures on the dark side of medicine.* Boston, MA: Beacon Press.

Farkas, J. 2015. Dear NEJM: We both know that conflicts of interest matter. *Pulmcrit Blog*, May 31. https://emcrit.org/pulmcrit/dear-nejm-we-both-know-that-conflicts-of-interest-matter/. Accessed January 24, 2018.

Freidson, E. 1970. *The profession of medicine: A study of the sociology of applied knowledge.* New York, NY: Dodd, Mead.

Glaser, B.E., and L.A. Bero. 2005. Attitudes of academic and clinical researchers toward financial ties in research: A systematic review. *Science and Engineering Ethics* 11(4): 553–573.

Godlee, F. 2015. Conflict of interest: Forward not backward. *BMJ* 350: h3176.

Grundy, Q., L. Tierney, C. Mayes, and W. Lipworth. 2017. Health professionals "make their choice": Pharmaceutical industry leaders' understandings of conflict of interest. *Journal of Bioethical Inquiry* 14(4): 541–553.

Healy, D. 2012. *Pharmageddon*. Berkeley, CA and Los Angeles, CA: University of California Press.

Horton, R. 2015. Offline: The BMJ vs NEJM—Lessons for us all. *The Lancet* 385(9984): 2238.

Institute of Medicine Committee on Conflict of Interest in Medical Research, Education, and Practices. 2009. *Conflict of interest in medical research, education, and practice*. Washington, DC: National Academies Press. www.ncbi.nlm.nih.gov/books/NBK22937/. Accessed October 10, 2015.

Leahey, E., and K. Montgomery. 2011. The meaning of regulation in a changing academic profession. In *The American academic profession: Changing forms and functions*, edited by Joseph Hermanowicz, 295–311. Baltimore, MD: Johns Hopkins University Press.

Lenzer, J., and S. Brownlee. 2015. Diverting attention from financial conflicts of interest. *BMJ* 350: h3505.

Lipworth, W., K. Montgomery, and M. Little. 2013. How pharmaceutical industry employees manage competing moral commitments. *Journal of Bioethical Inquiry* 10(3): 355–367.

Loder, E., C. Brizzell, and F. Godlee. 2015. Revisiting the commercial: Academic interface in medical journals. *BMJ* 350: h2957.

Lundh, A., S. Sismondo, J. Lexchin, O. Busuioc, and L. Bero. 2012. Industry sponsorship and research outcome. *Cochrane Database of Systematic Reviews* 12.

McCarthy, M. 2015. New England Journal of Medicine reconsiders relationship with industry. *BMJ* 350: h2575.

Miller, S. 2009. *The moral foundations of social institutions: A philosophical study*. New York, NY: Cambridge University Press.

Molchan, S. 2015. Criticism of NEJM's defense of industry: Physician relations. *Health News Review Blog*, May 14. www.healthnewsreview.org/2015/05/criticism-of-nejms-defense-of-industry-physician-relations/. Accessed January 23, 2018.

Morse, J.M. 1994. "Emerging from the data": The cognitive processes of analysis in qualitative inquiry. In *Critical issues in qualitative research methods*, edited by J.M. Morse, 23–43. Thousand Oaks, CA, London and New Delhi: Sage Publications.

Norris, S.L., H.K. Holmer, L.A. Ogden, S.S. Selph, and R. Fu. 2012. Conflict of interest disclosures for clinical practice guidelines in the national guideline clearinghouse. *PLoS ONE* 7(11): e47343.

Prasad, V. 2015. Why Lisa Rosenbaum gets conflict of interest policies wrong. *Lown Institute Blog*, May 28. http://lowninstitute.org/news/why-lisa-rosenbaum-gets-conflict-of-interest-policies-wrong/. Accessed January 23, 2018.

Prosser, H., S. Almond, and T. Walley. 2003. Influence on GPs' decision to prescribe new drugs: The importance of who says what. *Family Practice* 20(1): 61–68.

Rockey, S.J., and F.S. Collins. 2010. Managing financial conflict of interest in biomedical research. *JAMA* 303(23): 2400–2402.

Rodwin, M.A. 2012. Conflicts of interest, institutional corruption, and pharma: An agenda for reform. *Journal of Law, Medicine and Ethics* 40(3): 511–522.

Rosenbaum, L. 2015a. Beyond moral outrage: Weighing the trade-offs of COI regulation. *New England Journal of Medicine* 372(21): 2064–2068.

———. 2015b. Reconnecting the dots: Reinterpreting industry–Physician relations. *New England Journal of Medicine* 372(19): 1860–1864.

———. 2015c. Understanding bias: The case for careful study. *New England Journal of Medicine* 372(20): 1959–1963.

Scott, W.R. 2014. *Institutions and organizations*, 4th ed. Los Angeles, CA, London, New Delhi, Singapore and Washington, DC: Sage Publications.

Shaywitz, D., and T. Stossel. 2009. It's time to fight the "pharmascolds." *The Wall Street Journal*, April 8. www.wsj.com/articles/SB123914780537299005. Accessed October 13, 2015.

Steensma, D.P. 2015. Key opinion leaders. *Journal of Clinical Oncology* 33(28): 3213–3214.

Steinbrook, R. 2011. Future directions in industry funding of continuing medical education. *Archives of Internal Medicine* 171(3): 257–258.

Steinbrook, R., J.P. Kassirer, and M. Angell. 2015. Justifying conflicts of interest in medical journals: A very bad idea. *BMJ* 350: h2942.

Steinman, M.A., C.S. Landefeld, and R.B. Baron. 2012. Industry support of CME: Are we at the tipping point? *New England Journal of Medicine* 366(12): 1069–1071.

Stell, L.K. 2010. Avoiding over-deterrence in managing physicians' relationships with industry. *American Journal of Bioethics* 10(1): 27–29.

Steneck, N.H. 1999. Confronting misconduct in science in the 1980s and 1990s: What has and has not been accomplished? *Science and Engineering Ethics* 5(2): 161–175.

Stone, K. 2015. NEJM reignites conflict-of-interest debate with reader poll. *Health News Review*, June 2. www.healthnewsreview.org/2015/06/nejm-reignites-conflict-of-interest-debate-with-reader-poll/. Accessed March 07, 2018.

Stossel, T.P., and L.K. Stell. 2011. Time to "walk the walk" about industry ties to enhance health. *Nature Medicine* 17(4): 437–438.

Taitsman, J.K. 2011. Educating physicians to prevent fraud, waste, and abuse. *New England Journal of Medicine* 364(2): 102–103.

Williams, J., C. Mayes, P. Komesaroff, I. Kerridge, and W. Lipworth. 2017. Conflicts of interest in medicine: Taking diversity seriously. *Internal Medicine Journal* 47(7): 739–746.

Zinner, D.E., C.M. DesRoches, M.S.J. Bristol, B. Claridge, and E.G. Campbell. 2010. Tightening conflict-of-interest policies: The impact of 2005 ethics rules at the NIH. *Academic Medicine* 85(11): 1685–1691.

6 Medical Professionals as Expert Advisors in Macroallocation

Problems of Dual Agency and Conflict of Interest

Siun Gallagher

Background

In health systems that are, at least in part, regulated and funded by government, it is almost universal to conceptualize healthcare resources as scarce and in need of rationing (Light and Hughes 2001) and to have in place formal processes for distributing funds to healthcare programmes in accordance with their priority (Whitty and Littlejohns 2015; Landwehr and Klinnert 2015; Rumbold et al. 2017). In this analysis (part of a larger qualitative study of the ethical dimensions of doctors' involvement with policy concerning the allocation of healthcare resources), I report on the role-related conflicts of doctors who participate as technical experts in such macroallocation processes.

Macroallocation concerns decisions about the amount of resources available for particular kinds of health services and programmes (Scheunemann and White 2011; Kilner 2004; Bærøe 2008). It is distinguished from microallocation, or bedside rationing, by its focus on the healthcare needs of populations at an aggregate level and its locus at the level of governments and institutions. Because macroallocation generally entails normative assessments of the needs of groups of patients (Bærøe 2008) and choices between competing policy goals (Daniels 2016), it is often conceptualized as priority setting (Klein, Day, and Redmayne 1996; Kilner 2004).

Macroallocation processes usually employ the advice and knowledge of technical experts. These experts participate in devising options and formulating recommendations to decision-makers, who are often politicians but who may be local boards or executives, depending on the scale of the decision and the degree to which authority is delegated in the system. In western democracies, doctors dominate this advisory role (Belcher 2014; Duckett 1984; Kenny and Joffres 2008; Homan 2004; Martin, Abelson, and Singer 2002). That they are essential as expert informants seems to be generally accepted in practice (Whitty and Littlejohns 2015; Landwehr 2010).

The impartial expert assisting government has long been a recognized professional role available to doctors (Gillon 1986), although it is only recently that participation in the allocation of resources has come to be considered part of the doctor's job (Tilburt 2014). Encouraged by the influential "Medical Professionalism in the New Millennium: A Physician Charter" (ABIM Foundation 2004), in recent decades a growing number of codes of medical ethics across the globe have moved to represent advocacy for social justice, access to care, and the fair distribution of resources as a commitment of each individual doctor (Huddle 2011; Earnest, Wong, and Federico 2010; Tilburt 2014). The Australian Medical Association's urging of doctors to "use [their] knowledge and skills to assist those responsible for allocating healthcare resources, advocating for their transparent and equitable allocation" is a typical example of this move towards entrenching social responsibility and, along with it, medical influence over resource allocation, in the ethos of medicine (Australian Medical Association 2017, ¶4.4.3). How these obligations can be made to fit together with traditional professional commitments, most notably responsibilities to individual patients, has yet to be resolved (Tilburt 2014).

This change to the ideals of medical professionalism has prompted examination of the ethics of doctors' involvement in socially engaged actions by a small group of academics, notably Croft et al. (2012), Huddle (2011), Earnest, Wong, and Federico (2010), and Tilburt (2014). This literature characterizes the *ethical challenges* of doctors' performance of socially engaged roles such as priority setting, as: (1) their lack of special expertise in determining the outcomes likely to promote social justice (Huddle 2013a, 2014; McKie et al. 2008), (2) their limitations as barometers of public preferences (Thistlethwaite and Spencer 2008; Huddle 2013b), and (3) the role-related issues of conflict of interest and dual agency (Kerridge, Lowe, and Stewart 2013; Croft et al. 2012; Williams 2005; Smith et al. 2014; Huddle 2014).

Huddle (2011), who is a major critic of the promotion of medical involvement in resource allocation as a professional commitment, claims that its purpose of consolidating medical influence over healthcare resourcing is highly morally problematic and rightly invokes society's scepticism. Tilburt (2014) is more concerned with how to reconcile the new professional commitment to participation in distributive justice at macro and micro levels with the traditional medical ethical tenets that reflect the primacy of the doctor–patient contract.

The small available body of empirical literature on participants' experiences in macroallocation confirms that conflict of interest (McKie et al. 2008; Martin, Giacomini, and Singer 2002) and dual agency (Gallego, Fowler, and van Gool 2008; de Kort et al. 2007) are ethical issues that arise in this setting.

Conflict of interest is said to exist in circumstances where there is a possibility that secondary interests—including financial benefits and opportunities for professional progression, recognition, and influence—will influence actions and judgements concerning primary interests—such as patient care (Lo and Field 2009). In healthcare policymaking scholarship and practice, concern tends to be focused on financial conflicts; non-financial conflicts are more often accepted, even though their potential to assume higher priority than primary interests ensures that they are also deeply problematical (Kesselheim and Maisel 2010) (see also observations in Chapter 5 of this volume). Formal disclosure and monitoring policies are the most common means of dealing with the problem of conflict of interest. The cultivation of medical virtue has been proposed as an alternative remedy (DuBois et al. 2013; Oakley 2014, 669).

For salaried medical practitioners, who make up the majority of doctors providing public healthcare in Australia, remuneration is largely unrelated to the dimensions or complexity of the service. As a consequence, financial conflicts may be less important than non-financial conflicts. Because healthcare resource investments and disinvestments affect both the volume and form of services, they shape the nature and scope of professional practice (Smith et al. 2014), and thereby the opportunities available to doctors to excel clinically, build reputations, perform research, and appoint and develop staff, amongst other things. In the macroallocation setting, the concern is that such considerations, rather than results for patients or the community, could motivate doctors' contributions to policy deliberations (Croft et al. 2012). Doctors and others might consider such tensions to be innocent—for might not the needs of the patient, doctor, and staff all coalesce around the "better" service that results from new resources?—when in reality not all decisions benefit all parties equally. A service enhancement weighted towards research, for example, might benefit the doctor's reputation and distant future patients more than it meets the needs of current patients or helps society to address contemporary problems.

Dual agency might be viewed as a special form of conflict of interest. It is defined by Tilburt (2014) as an "avowed requirement to act simultaneously on behalf of two different parties with competing interests" (30). It is a feature of a number of branches of medicine, for example, military and occupational medicine, and of common medical tasks such as the certification of patients' fitness to drive; in such cases, the traditional tenet of medical professionalism—that the patient comes first—is challenged by the doctor's obligations to society, government, or a corporation. Priority setting of necessity entails dual agency, because it requires doctors whose primary professional interests are in patient care to provide neutral technical advice as an agent of government and in the interest of society and to conform to distributive justice-based principles, which are often incompatible with meeting individual patients' needs and desires (Pugh 2018). Indeed, it has been common for philosophers and economists to reject the notion that doctors have a legitimate role in resource allocation, arguing that their fiduciary duty to the patient is incompatible with representing community or national interests in the apportionment of resources (Cassel 1985; Kerridge, Lowe, and Stewart 2013; Wasserman and Wertheimer 2014). Dual agency might also play out when doctors have simultaneous commitments to assisting governments in the fair allocation of resources and to maximizing the resources available to their own healthcare organizations or practices.

Notwithstanding reservations about conflicts of interest and dual agency, doctors look set to remain embedded in the role of expert advisor in macroallocation—both because of the need for policy deliberation to be informed by doctors' unique experience and knowledge and because of the incorporation of a commitment to distributive justice into the ethos of medicine. Thus, exploring how doctors can navigate competing commitments is increasingly seen as an important area for medical ethics (Tilburt 2014; Tilburt and Brody 2016; Sabin 2000; Wasserman and Wertheimer 2014; Ross and Bernabeo 2014).

In such work, conflict of interest and dual agency are usually problematized more as ethical quandaries facing doctors than as threats to distributive justice. Consequently, suggested ethical frameworks for addressing the problem tend to be physician-focused—prescribing attitudes and actions for doctors to take. This approach overestimates both doctors' insight into potential conflicts and the degree to which they are troubled by them (Klugman 2017; DuBois 2017). More significantly, it overlooks the social context of macroallocation. Priority setting at this level occurs typically in a deliberative process that brings together a plurality of voices and skills to argue the merits of a range of claims and norms (Danziger 1995; Gottweis 2007; Majone 1989).

The privileged access doctors gain, whilst engaged in macroallocation, to opportunities to advance their careers and pursue patient-related interests prompted my interest in understanding whether and, if so, in what form doctors appreciate role-related conflict as an ethical issue. This component of the study aimed to expand the empirical knowledge base on doctors' experiences of ethical challenges in the role of the technical expert in priority setting, test some of the theoretical claims concerning conflict of interest and dual agency, and explore ethical frameworks that might guide doctors in this setting.

Empirical Observations

Study Setting

In order to obtain a rich picture of doctors' ethical intuitions and of their understanding of the social process of priority setting (Ives and Draper 2009; Ebbesen and Pedersen 2007), I designed a qualitative interview study of doctors who act as technical experts in macroallocation. The enquiry elicited reflection on the roles doctors play in policy and their practical experience of those roles. Using the principles of the constructivist empirical bioethics methodology known as grounded moral analysis (GMA) (Dunn et al. 2012), doctors' conceptual understandings were considered alongside ethical theory in order to arrive at an understanding of ethics in macroallocation work. The focus was on doctors who elected to engage in policy as individuals, rather than as nominees of interest groups (Contandriopoulos

2011) and whose interests were focused on the resourcing of services rather than on the rights of medical practitioners or broad professional reform.

Method

Interviews were conducted with twenty doctors, purposively selected on the basis that they had participated in policy concerning the allocation of funding to healthcare programmes at one or more levels of the healthcare system.

The study method was based on Charmaz's (2014) constructivist model of grounded theory, modified to accommodate the principles of grounded moral analysis (GMA), an iterative empirical bioethics methodology employing contemporaneous interchange between the ethical and empirical to support normative claims grounded in practice (Dunn et al. 2012).

The doctors in the sample were or had been (in the case of the small number who had retired) full-time or substantial part-time specialists or clinical academics employed in hospitals and universities in New South Wales, Australia. The distribution of age (average 58; range 38–80), sex (5 female, 15 male), and place of training in our sample mirrored the profile of the general cohort of specialist doctors in Australia (Australian Institute of Health and Welfare 2016, 2014).

A semi-structured interview format was used, with questions and prompts designed to elicit participants' experiences and encourage reflection on the ethical dimensions of the role. Participants were asked about competition for the health dollar; the roles they played in macroallocation; positive and negative experiences in the role; the characteristics, behaviours, and achievements of those of whom they approved and disapproved; and their views on how power and relationships were relevant to the policy process. If the information had not been otherwise elicited, they were probed to discuss aspects of the process that had caused them moral unease. Interviews averaged sixty-five minutes.

The interviews were audio-recorded and transcribed verbatim. Inductive and abductive data analysis was undertaken progressively from the commencement of the interviews. As the analysis progressed, it became obvious that justice and self-efficacy were of deep concern to the participants, suggesting virtue ethics as an appropriate ethical lens through which to examine the phenomenon. In keeping with the GMA methodology described by Dunn and colleagues (2012), the interview schedule was modified in two iterations to draw out experiences that responded to this theory.

Results

Participants in the study gave accounts of acting in the expert role in macroallocation at one or more levels, from institution based to international, with most engaging in multiple macroallocation processes and jurisdictions, either in parallel or over the course of a career. Participants' actions in priority setting included membership of committees, attendance at meetings with decision-makers, lobbying, construction of independent processes designed to advance policy debate, and preparation of submissions, applications, and correspondence. They contributed expert advice to decisions about whether specific health service programmes would receive funding or, if already funded, enhanced funding. These activities were undertaken as individual health service employees rather than as members of medical interest groups.

Participants did not immediately recognize role-related conflict in macroallocation as an ethical issue or find it troubling; in fact, they were more concerned about the ethical ramifications of procedural deficiencies, such as bureaucratic inefficiency and behaviours and structures that disadvantage certain types of participant. Nevertheless, their accounts showed that the expert role entailed both conflict of interest and dual agency, as described ahead, followed by participants' views on strategies to manage these conflicts.

Conflicts of Interest

While participants spoke in detail about their engagement in processes for managing conflict of interest, they largely denied being influenced by either the desire for personal financial gain, or the desire to progress their careers; rather, it was common for them to claim to be the "champions" of their services, engaging in macroallocation to enhance their quality, reputation, and resourcing:

> Most health is about "my disease is bigger than your disease" and if you do a cost-of-illness study, everyone's disease is the biggest and all of that, but my prime motivation was actually for advocacy for [my specialty] because they are the poor cousin.

Participants thus offered melioristic motives for their own involvement with macroallocation, such as a desire to provide "the best service possible."

Yet that these motives may coexist with more self-seeking motives was suggested by their accounts of their career trajectories. Of the twenty participants, eleven had entered an emerging specialty or subspecialty or had identified and developed their practices to focus on a previously unrecognized issue; almost all of the remainder occupied niches in evolving areas of their specialties. Universally, they expressed considerable personal pride and satisfaction about their success in amassing resources and developing their services in terms of size, reputation, and status. One participant acknowledged, and rationalized, this dual purpose:

> I think people who say they have never had an ethical dilemma lie or they don't reflect. I'm a little bit in the non-reflecting [group] now because I am 100 per cent sure that I would've advocated, hopefully for the right thing but with somewhere an ulterior motive, and that's really an

ethical dilemma, I'm pretty sure. And for me, it's a very uneasy feeling obviously, and I think it comes to the point where I then hope that what I achieve to advocate is worth more than what my ulterior motive was, to tell yourself, oh, I'll be OK.

While denying that they themselves had conflicts of interest, participants argued that it was inevitable that *other* doctors who engage in macroallocation might have some degree of conflict of interest:

> Clearly you have to be careful that you're not self-serving, all right? And I guess in medicine like everywhere else, there are a whole heap of individuals, some of whom will be out to benefit number one, themselves, rather than the system. But apart from being aware of that and avoiding that in my own behaviour and trying to be objective and fair, I've seen that in other people sometimes, and that's been of concern, but that's how humans are.

This sentiment was echoed strongly by other participants, who showed disapproval of colleagues who engaged in macroallocation activities for self-serving reasons—for example, as a means of building an empire or developing a career:

> That whole idea that those roles are simply one more step in your career I find deeply offensive. Deeply offensive.

Although participants thought badly of colleagues who used their macroallocation roles for personal, career, or other benefits, they were less critical of people with intellectual biases (i.e. biases stemming from a commitment to a particular line of reasoning). In fact, several objected to the practice of excluding the views of individuals because of their prior work on a drug, device, or service that was under consideration. They considered that intellectual conflict of interest, even though problematic, was the price that had to be paid for expertise: a person ignorant of the detail of the policy area would be neither interested in participating nor useful. They believed that having a number of different expert voices in the room mitigated the risk of a decision being swayed by someone with a conflict of interest:

> Conflict of interest. I think where it's known, I think it's better to use people with—and recognize their conflicts of interest [rather] than just to exclude them and have a whole bunch of people that don't know anything about it.

Dual Agency

A substantial number of the doctors in the sample characterized themselves as protectors of the national purse. They were concerned about transparency, accountability, and waste in the health sector. For these doctors, engaging with practical matters of distributive justice was a natural response to those concerns and a legitimate role for them and for doctors generally, to play.

> You're making decisions about allocation of the healthcare dollar in a cost-effective and equitable way—so that is, in a way, you're advocating for patients but you're also advocating nationally for the country—so it's not so much advocacy, but being at the pointy end of the way health care dollars are being allocated.

They believed in their own capacity to act in society's interests and were confident that, without doctors' experience and perspectives, decision-making would be impossible:

> So I think that the system needs societal good, all right? And we probably have enough ego to believe that we can do—we can prescribe what that looks like.

Dual agency was represented in participants' experiences of a conflict between their fiduciary duty to individual patients and the macroallocation roles they undertook as agents of the state. Some participants described the problem at a conceptual level:

> It's the classic tension between the public good and the individual good and in that setting you can see it.

Many more gave accounts of their propensity to advocate for the patients under their care, even in situations where they were conscious that their role was to provide dispassionate expert advice:

> Presenting the data, I always had to say I have to declare [that] my conflict here is that I really want this drug for my patients, it could make a big difference, but obviously they're costly.

Participants fell into two groups in the way they experienced and dealt with dual agency. The first declared no difficulty in separating their roles in macroallocation from their obligations to individual patients. They often spoke about the different "hats" they wore for different purposes, or about "compartmentalizing" themselves:

> I think it has to be someone who's interested in societal health and being an advocate for society because you've got to switch hats; if you're a clinician and you're treating a patient then clearly your role is to advocate for that patient and they would quite reasonably not like it if you took a societal view, [you] try and get the best you can for that patient, but if you're making decisions you've got to put—take that hat off and put a

different hat on, and most clinicians don't like doing that; they stay in the clinical mould.

Well at a personal level, I never found it that—I didn't feel conflicted about it. Because when you've got a patient in front of you, what you're doing is, whatever is appropriate for that patient and that's regardless of whether there are resources there or not. You'd go and get the resources if you can, or use everything that's available to you. At a policy level, you're looking at more generic broader issues and I don't think—again I don't think that's in conflict with doing everything you can for the patient or everything appropriate for the patient in front of you.

The second group actively sought to serve the interests of their specialty's patients whilst engaged with macroallocation tasks on behalf of the state:

But each person would make different contributions in different fields. The oncologist would be very much advocating for oncology patients and tending to push the idea that that would get through. I would be tending to push the idea that [drugs relevant to my specialty] should get up, although sometimes I didn't think they should.

Participants in this group believed favouring one's own specialty was a necessary evil, reasoning that a totally disinterested person would not engage in deliberations about policy or contribute meaningfully:

Supposedly at that time I was working for the government, but yeah, I was making sure that we got a good deal for the people I was kind of advocating for because why else would I be on it? So I had dual purpose but trying to work in with their regulations. So I don't know. I didn't feel badly about it.

Some participants were critical of colleagues with medico-political role conflicts, which were evident when doctors advanced medical professional concerns—for example, enhancing doctors' remuneration levels and protecting professional "turf"—in parallel with or instead of the societal interests to which they were expected to restrict their contributions.

Managing Role-Related Conflict

Participants understood the constraints on their influence in the deliberative processes in which they engaged and were confident that the bureaucratic and political procedures surrounding decision-making could correctly manage conflicts of interest and dual agency. One participant, an advisor to a wide range of local and national policy processes, expressed succinctly a theme that was strongly present throughout the data—"Even if it's not an outcome I agree with, if the process is fair then I'm happy with that."

The plurality of views taken into account in macroallocation was held by some to be a safeguard against opinions motivated by conflicts holding sway:

> And probably you deal with it by having a few experts, because even if they have conflicts they're undoubtedly going to be different conflicts, and they'll have different perspectives, and you can't get two experts to agree on very much anyway.

Participants indicated satisfaction with the common strategies used for managing conflicts—declarations of conflicts of interest, transparency, and self-monitoring—although most considered that such strategies were not implemented with sufficient rigour. Participants also reported that doctors engaged in self-policing strategies, such as weeding out peers who pursued medico-political or ideological goals and calling out colleagues who blatantly or consistently offered partisan arguments:

> I think, probably for everyone to be open to that idea about themselves and others and to call it more and say, "hang on, mate, that seems a bit sectoral." So, I think honesty in our exchanges—like most of us have got a pretty good antenna for this sort of stuff and you can hear the corporate speak and the—it's all over the place.

Discussion

The data in this study showed that both conflicts of interest and dual agency were features of macroallocation practice: in the technical expert role, agency on behalf of society had the potential to conflict with doctors' personal goals for career and financial advancement and with their duties to the patients and patient groups for which they were responsible as clinicians, lending support to the claims made in the theoretical and empirical literatures about the phenomenon of role-related conflicts in priority setting.

However, doctors did not view these phenomena as ethically relevant at a personal level. Few of the doctors recognized their own conflicts of interest or appreciated the claims such conflicts make on medical virtue and procedural justice. This was predictable, because it is a property of conflict of interest that those it affects underestimate both its potential to influence their choices (Klugman 2017; DuBois 2017) and the difficulties involved in managing it (Mayes, Lipworth, and Kerridge 2016).

It was surprising, however, that respondents also were insensitive to the risk associated with dual agency, even though the phenomenon was highly visible to them: those who claimed facility in giving primacy to societal interests and those who knowingly tried to achieve benefits for both patients and society were equally confident in the defensibility and success of their chosen approach.

Importantly, neither of these conflicts weighed on participants as ethical issues or caused them moral unease. Although these doctors were concerned about the justice of the decisions in which they were involved—and disapproved of the impact of others' conflicts on the conduct and outcomes of priority setting processes—they had few intimations that their own behaviours might be transgressive or that their behaviours might be viewed as such by others. This finding suggests that if we are to continue to conceptualize role-related conflicts in resource allocation as a problem, we need to be more specific about how and by whom the problem is experienced and its consequences felt. That is, the data do not support the idea that role-related conflict troubles doctors at the level of their internal professional ethical landscapes. This finding runs counter to the ethics frameworks that have been advanced to address the perceived problem.

It is common for codes of medical ethics and scholars writing in this area to assume that the technical expert role entails, at least to some extent, acting on behalf of patients or causes, and, thereby to conceptualize expert advice-giving as a form of physician advocacy (Bagshaw and Barnett 2017; Gruen, Campbell, and Blumenthal 2006). A prominent thread in this study showed that many doctors strongly identified with being an agent of society, rather than a patient advocate, when engaging in macroallocation. The plurality of motivations and values shown by participants suggests that the expert advisor role does not fit neatly under the "physician advocacy" umbrella. Continuing to conflate the two may risk perpetuating misunderstandings about the function of the technical expert in policymaking. Further disambiguation of the concepts of "expert" and "advocate" in this setting would be helpful to those seeking to define medical professionalism and offer ethical guidance to doctors.

This study's other salient finding was participants' confidence that the social processes of macroallocation would effectively manage role-related conflicts. The doctors in this study were willing participants in and keen supporters of the standard mitigation strategies for conflict of interest, which are largely focused on financial conflicts (Lo and Field 2009); they were critical when these strategies were imperfectly implemented and took action to curtail the partisanship of others. Conflicts were not suffered internally, or hidden; rather, they were displayed openly so that they could be viewed, evaluated, and responded to by the other participants in the process. This pattern suggests that participants had a sophisticated understanding of the social role of "expert" within the practical world of policymaking. Their recognition of the communitarian aims of macroallocation and conceptualization of role-related conflicts at the collective, rather than the individual, level enabled them to cede to the group the responsibility for managing the impact of conflicts on the fairness of resource distributions. This legitimization of the power of the group opens up opportunities for defining the problem of role-related conflict and exploring its implications and management in a social context.

On the basis of these findings, it can be hypothesized that doctors who engage in macroallocation experience role-related conflict not as a problem of professional ethics but as a normal part of the social process of priority setting. Thus, in health systems that are, at least in part, regulated and funded by government, doctors' professional positioning as parts of institutions may set the scene for their recognition of macroallocation as a cooperative endeavour and its problems as social phenomena that require a collective response.

Mitigation strategies for dual agency usually take as their starting point the doctor as an individual, who must navigate an internal landscape in which duty to the patient is pitted against duty to the community and those who have commissioned the doctor's advice. The most compelling approach that has yet been offered to the problem of dual agency relies on role ethics, in which duty to society is assigned to specific medical roles. Doctors may occupy these roles from time to time, as needed (Tilburt 2014), or the roles may be assigned to selected doctors, who will occupy them continuously on behalf of others (Tilburt and Brody 2016). Its critics claim, broadly, that "that's not how things work" and that, for a doctor in this position, accepting the "complex algorithm" that is professionalism may be the only way to reconcile competing commitments (Ubel 2014; Ross and Bernabeo 2014; Wasserman and Wertheimer 2014).

This demonstration of doctors' deficiency in the reflexivity necessary for discerning and responding at a personal level to role-related conflict lends weight to the arguments of those who are sceptical about the potential of role ethics to offer a solution to dual agency. In addition, the findings demonstrating the value doctors place on the social processes of macroallocation that safeguard procedural fairness lend support to traditional oversight-based approaches to conflict of interest. Together, these findings suggest that the preoccupation in the medical ethics literature with the doctor's interior ethical landscape may be ill founded and that the problem and its solutions lie in the social world.

Medical ethical frameworks founded on communitarian principles might, thus, better illuminate the problem than physician-centred frameworks such as role ethics and virtue ethics that rely on doctors' self-awareness and reflexivity. Practical solutions to the ethical challenges inherent in the technical expert role might be found in institutional approaches that focus on safeguarding procedural justice through transparency and external checks and balances and encompass all professional disciplines. An example of a system that would lend itself to this purpose is the "accountability for reasonableness" (A4R) ethical framework (Daniels and Sabin 1997). The framework's four conditions—relevance, publicity or transparency, the possibility of appeals and revision, and regulative/enforcement mechanisms—support the operationalization of fairness in macroallocation.

Implications for Practice

If the problems of dual agency and conflict of interest do not trouble doctors who engage in macroallocation, ethical approaches that are premised on resolution of physician ethical unease are unnecessary. They also can be a distraction from the true ethical problem of how the collective of individuals involved in macroallocation processes might best discharge its responsibilities for procedural justice. Medical ethics scholars might, therefore, consider broadening the scope of their enquiry to acknowledge the social nature of macroallocation.

Codes of medical ethics that enjoin doctors to take up opportunities to engage in resource allocation are often criticized for failing to provide the action guide that will enable doctors who do so to reconcile the competing commitments it entails. An approach to filling this gap that would be consistent with these findings would be for the codes to (1) promote sensitivity to context (Ross and Bernabeo 2014), (2) encourage doctors to become familiar with and recognize the qualities of pluralistic policy development models and their participants (Cassel 1985), and (3) emphasize the need to approach the task with humility and collegiality.

At a practical level, macroallocation institutions might draw comfort from these data showing doctors' appetite for procedural approaches to the management of role-related conflict and redouble their efforts in implementing frameworks designed to safeguard procedural justice at a holistic level.

Conclusion

As perhaps the first study to describe the role-related conflicts encountered by doctors when engaging in macroallocation as technical experts, these findings confirm the long theorized problems of conflict of interest and dual agency. Interestingly, doctors in this sample constructed role-related conflict not as a challenge to medical professional ethics but as part of the social process of priority setting. Although participants showed an underdeveloped appreciation of the threats these conflicts pose to medical virtue and procedural justice, they were confident that the institution of macroallocation would protect them and the community from significant harm.

The common tendency to construct role-related conflict as a professional ethics matter and to seek solutions in medical virtue and role ethics is not supported by this analysis. That doctors conceptualize the problem as existing in the social, rather than internal, world suggests that procedural justice ethics frameworks may offer both a more fertile setting for the exploration of the ethical implications of role-related conflicts and a more viable approach to safeguarding distributive justice in priority setting from its consequences.

References

ABIM Foundation. 2004. *Medical professionalism in the new millennium: A physicians' charter*, September 2. www.abimfoundation.org/what-we-do/physician-charter. Accessed February 1, 2018.

Australian Institute of Health and Welfare. 2014. Medical workforce 2012. In *National health workforce series*. Canberra: AIHW.

———. 2016. *Australia's medical workforce 2015*. Canberra: AIHW.

Australian Medical Association. 2017. *AMA code of ethics 2004. Editorially revised 2006. Revised 2016*. Australian Medical Association. ama.com.au/position-state ment/ama-code-ethics-2004-editorially-revised-2006. Accessed April 22, 2017.

Bærøe, K. 2008. Priority setting in health care: On the relation between reasonable choices on the micro-level and the macro-level. *Theoretical Medicine and Bioethics* 29(2): 87.

Bagshaw, P., and P. Barnett. 2017. Physician advocacy in Western medicine: A 21st century challenge. *The New Zealand Medical Journal* 130(1466): 83–89.

Belcher, H. 2014. Power, politics and health care. In *Second opinion: An introduction to health sociology*, edited by J. Germov, 356–379. Melbourne: Oxford University Press.

Cassel, C.K. 1985. Doctors and allocation decisions: A new role in the new medicare. *Journal of Health Politics, Policy and Law* 10(3): 549–564.

Charmaz, K. 2014. *Constructing grounded theory*. London: Sage Publications.

Contandriopoulos, D. 2011. On the nature and strategies of organized interests in health care policy making. *Administration & Society* 43(1): 45–65.

Croft, D., S.J. Jay, E.M. Meslin, M.M. Gaffney, and J.D. Odell. 2012. Perspective: Is it time for advocacy training in medical education? *Academic Medicine* 87(9): 1165–1170.

Daniels, N. 2016. Resource allocation and priority setting. In *Public health ethics: Cases spanning the globe*, edited by D.H. Barrett, L.H. Ortmann, A. Dawson, C. Saenz, A. Reis, and G. Bolan. Cham: Springer International Publishing.

Daniels, N., and J. Sabin. 1997. Limits to health care: Fair procedures, democratic deliberation and the legitimacy problems for insurers. *Philosophy and Public Affairs* 26(4): 303–350.

Danziger, M. 1995. Policy analysis postmodernized. *Policy Studies Journal* 23(3): 435–450.

de Kort, S.J., N. Kenny, P. van Dijk, S. Gevers, D.J. Richel, and D.L. Willems. 2007. Cost issues in new disease-modifying treatments for advanced cancer: In-depth interviews with physicians. *European Journal of Cancer* 43(13): 1983–1989.

DuBois, J.M. 2017. Physician decision making and the web of influence. *The American Journal of Bioethics* 17(6): 24–26.

DuBois, J.M., E.M. Kraus, A.A. Mikulec, S. Cruz-Flores, and E. Bakanas. 2013. A humble task: Restoring virtue in an age of conflicted interests. *Academic Medicine* 88(7): 924–928.

Duckett, S.J. 1984. Special issue: Health and health care in Australasia structural interests and Australian health policy. *Social Science & Medicine* 18(11): 959–966.

Dunn, M., M. Sheehan, T. Hope, and M. Parker. 2012. Toward methodological innovation in empirical ethics research. *Cambridge Quarterly of Healthcare Ethics* 21(4): 466–480.

Earnest, M.A., S.L. Wong, and S.G. Federico. 2010. Perspective: Physician advocacy: What is it and how do we do it? *Academic Medicine* 85(1): 63–67.

Ebbesen, M., and B.D. Pedersen. 2007. Using empirical research to formulate normative ethical principles in biomedicine. *Medicine, Health Care and Philosophy* 10(1): 33–48.

Gallego, G., S. Fowler, and K. van Gool. 2008. Decision makers' perceptions of health technology decision making and priority setting at the institutional level. *Australian Health Review* 32(3): 520–527.

Gillon, R. 1986. *Philosophical medical ethics.* Chichester: Wiley.

Gottweis, H. 2007. Rhetoric in policy making: Between logos, ethos, and pathos. In *Handbook of public policy analysis: Theory, politics & methods*, edited by F. Fischer, G.J. Miller, and M.S. Sidney. Boca Raton, FL: Taylor & Francis.

Gruen, R.L., E.G. Campbell, and D. Blumenthal. 2006. Public roles of US physicians: Community participation, political involvement, and collective advocacy. *JAMA* 296(20): 2467–2475.

Homan, M.S. 2004. *Promoting community change: Making it happen in the real world*, Vol. 3. Belmont, CA: Thomson, Brooks, Cole.

Huddle, T.S. 2011. Perspective: Medical professionalism and medical education should not involve commitments to political advocacy. *Academic Medicine* 86(3): 378–383.

———. 2013a. The limits of social justice as an aspect of medical professionalism. *Journal of Medicine and Philosophy* 38(4): 369–387.

———. 2013b. The limits of social justice as an aspect of medical professionalism. *The Journal of Medicine and Philosophy* 38(4): 369–387.

———. 2014. Political activism is not mandated by medical professionalism. *American Journal of Bioethics* 14(9): 51–53.

Ives, J., and H. Draper. 2009. Appropriate methodologies for empirical bioethics: It's all relative. *Bioethics* 23(4): 249–258.

Kenny, N., and C. Joffres. 2008. An ethical analysis of international health priority-setting. *Health Care Analysis* 16(2): 145–160.

Kerridge, I.H., M. Lowe, and C. Stewart. 2013. *Ethics and law for the health professions.* Annandale, NSW: The Federation Press.

Kesselheim, A.S., and W.H. Maisel. 2010. Managing financial and nonfinancial conflicts of interest in healthcare delivery. *American Journal of Therapeutics* 17(4): 440–443.

Kilner, J.F. 2004. Healthcare resources, allocation of: I. Macroallocation. In *Encyclopedia of bioethics*, edited by S.G. Post, 1098–1107. New York, NY: Macmillan Reference USA.

Klein, R., P. Day, and S. Redmayne. 1996. *Managing scarcity: Priority setting and rationing in the National Health Service.* Buckingham: Open University Press.

Klugman, C. 2017. Shining light on conflicts of interest. *The American Journal of Bioethics* 17(6): 1–3.

Landwehr, C. 2010. Democratic and technocratic policy deliberation. *Critical Policy Studies* 3(3–4): 434–439.

Landwehr, C., and D. Klinnert. 2015. Value congruence in health care priority setting: Social values, institutions and decisions in three countries. *Health Economics, Policy and Law* 10(2): 113–132.

Light, D.W., and D. Hughes. 2001. Introduction: A sociological perspective on rationing: Power, rhetoric and situated practices. *Sociology of Health & Illness* 23(5): 551–569.

Lo, B., and M.J. Field. 2009. *Conflict of interest in medical research, education, and practice.* Washington, DC: National Academies Press.

Majone, G. 1989. *Evidence, argument, and persuasion in the policy process.* New Haven, CT: Yale University Press.

Martin, D., J. Abelson, and P. Singer. 2002. Participation in health care priority-setting through the eyes of the participants. *Journal of Health Services Research & Policy* 7(4): 222–229.

Martin, D., M. Giacomini, and P. Singer. 2002. Fairness, accountability for reasonableness, and the views of priority setting decision-makers. *Health Policy* 61(3): 279–290.

Mayes, C., W. Lipworth, and I. Kerridge. 2016. Declarations, accusations and judgement: Examining conflict of interest discourses as performative speech-acts. *Medicine, Health Care and Philosophy* 19(3): 455–462.

McKie, J., B. Shrimpton, R. Hurworth, C. Bell, and J. Richardson. 2008. Who should be involved in health care decision making? A qualitative study. *Health Care Analysis* 16(2): 114–126.

Oakley, J. 2014. A virtue ethics analysis of disclosure requirements and financial incentives as responses to conflicts of interest in physician prescribing. In *The future of bioethics: International dialogues*, edited by A. Akabayashi, 669–676. Oxford: Oxford University Press.

Pugh, J. 2018. Navigating individual and collective interests in medical ethics. *Journal of Medical Ethics* 44(1): 1–2.

Ross, K.M., and E. Bernabeo. 2014. When professional obligations collide: Context matters. *American Journal of Bioethics* 14(9): 38–40.

Rumbold, B., R. Baker, O. Ferraz, et al. 2017. Universal health coverage, priority setting, and the human right to health. *The Lancet* 390(10095): 712–714.

Sabin, J.E. 2000. Fairness as a problem of love and the heart: A clinician's perspective on priority setting. In *The global challenge of health care rationing*, edited by A. Coulter and C. Ham. Philadelphia, PA: Open University Press.

Scheunemann, L.P., and D.B. White. 2011. The ethics and reality of rationing in medicine. *Chest* 140(6): 1625–1632.

Smith, N., C. Mitton, A. Davidson, and I. Williams. 2014. A politics of priority setting: Ideas, interests and institutions in healthcare resource allocation. *Public Policy and Administration* 29(4): 331–347.

Thistlethwaite, J., and J. Spencer. 2008. *Professionalism in medicine*. Oxford: Radcliffe Publishing.

Tilburt, J.C. 2014. Addressing dual agency: Getting specific about the expectations of professionalism. *American Journal of Bioethics* 14(9): 29–36.

Tilburt, J.C., and B. Brody. 2016. Doubly distributing special obligations: What professional practice can learn from parenting. *Journal of Medical Ethics* 44: 212–216.

Ubel, P.A. 2014. Agency is messy: Get used to it. *American Journal of Bioethics* 14(9): 37–38.

Wasserman, D., and A. Wertheimer. 2014. In defense of bunkering. *American Journal of Bioethics* 14(9): 42–43.

Whitty, J.A., and P. Littlejohns. 2015. Social values and health priority setting in Australia: An analysis applied to the context of health technology assessment. *Health Policy* 119(2): 127–136.

Williams, J.R. 2005. *Medical ethics manual*. Cedex, France: World Medical Association.

Part III

Reconceptualization and Concluding Observations

7   After Dominance

The Elastic Politics of Medicine

Christopher Jordens

His fault, too great a love of humankind.

—Aeschylus, *Prometheus Bound*

Politics, Criticism, and Power

When it is used in connection with medicine, the term "politics" can mean different things. It can refer to power struggles within the profession or power struggles between the medical profession and other professions. It can refer to a kind of power exercised by medical experts over those who seek medical care or a kind of technological power over nature itself. It can refer to power struggles within and between different levels of government or different sectors of the economy, over the control of health services. The common factor in these examples is the concept of power. Taken in its most general sense, the politics of medicine ask questions about power: is there a form of power implicated in the theory and practice of medicine? If so, what does it look like? What are its effects on those who exercise it and on those upon whom it is exercised? I want to suggest that the politics of medicine exist alongside the ethics of medicine as an important—if perhaps less well theorized—means by which medicine deals with questions of value. One of the aims of this chapter is to help build a clearer picture of these politics by discussing what I take to be two of its manifestations. One is political criticism. The other is what I call "ideologies of care."

Since the 1960s, the profession of medicine has come under sustained political criticism. I will focus here on two lines of criticism which are both common and persistent but which differ in terms of their basic concerns and their chief protagonists. One calls medicine to account for its expansionist tendencies. In essence, this criticism is based on concerns about medicine "overreaching." Such concerns are as old as modernity and perhaps as old as Western civilization itself, but they have found expression in recent decades, particularly in the social sciences, as the *critique of medicalization*. The other line of criticism calls medicine to account for its reductionist tendencies. This critique is based on concerns about the effect of scientific knowledge on both the knower and the known, and it has been cultivated particularly, but by no means exclusively, in the humanities.

I will argue that these two criticisms are underpinned by different assumptions about the kind of power exercised by and through the profession of medicine. I will also argue that, even if they often occur together, these criticisms cut across each other or pull medicine in different directions: one tends to propel medicine into new "jurisdictions" or domains of life, whereas the other tends to hold it back. Following Zola (1972), I characterize the general directions or "vectors" of medicine's expansion into new jurisdictions. The concept of disease is widely understood to play an important role in this process, but I argue that its importance is diminishing, and therefore possibly overplayed. I highlight the expansionary influence of humanistic values that inform what I call "ideologies of care." These are prescriptive, ideal models of care that translate political criticism into norms of practice. Examples include "patient-centred care" and "evidence-based medicine," which feature in other chapters of this book.

In the following section I introduce a typology of concepts of power. In the section "Political Critiques of Medicine," I describe each of the critiques of medicine in detail. This section will highlight how Zola's (1972) original description of medicalization was *anomalous* with respect to the theories of power that were then current in the social sciences, and I suggest that it is a better fit for structural theories of power that emerged in the humanities. In the section "'Vectors' of Medicine's Expansion," following Zola, I trace the expansion of medicine into new jurisdictions, differentiating three different "vectors" of expansion on the basis of some philosophical distinctions. I conclude with some reflections on political criticism of medicine and ideologies of care, and I invite the reader to consider how the other chapters of this book highlight, in different ways, the effects of such ideologies on the experience of medical professionals.

Concepts of Power

There are many different ways to slice and dice concepts of power. I will draw here on a typology developed by Heiskala (2001) which distinguishes between *distributive*, *collective*, and *structural* approaches and associates each with a different theorist—that is, Weber, Parsons, and Foucault, respectively.

Heiskala takes Weber's (1978 [1922]) definition of power as a point of departure: "'power' is the probability that one actor within a social relationship will be in a position to carry out his own will despite resistance, regardless of the basis on which this probability rests" (2001, 242). Heiskala characterizes Weber's approach as *distributive* in that, in any given social relationship between *a* and *b*, power is "usually understood as a zero-sum game: an increase in *a*'s power means a corresponding decrease in *b*'s power, and vice versa" (243).

Distributive notions of power are enshrined in everyday English usage to the extent that we speak of power as something that some people "have" or "don't have" (i.e. those who are powerful or powerless, respectively).[1] It is also consistent with the idea that power is exercised by one individual or group *over* another. This kind of relationship is frequently glossed as "domination." Such notions of power can be understood as negative or interdictory as well as distributive in that domination obviates or limits the autonomy of the dominated party. This explains why critiques of dominance motivate strategies that aim to protect and increase the autonomy of the dominated party (as illustrated in Chapter 2).

Heiskala contrasts distributive approaches to power with a collective (Parsonian) approach, according to which

> *a* and *b* can in co-operation enhance their joint power over third parties and over nature. Power in this sense is no longer a zero-sum game but an emerging resource for *a* and *b* over *c*.
>
> (Heiskala 2001, 243)

Heiskala argues that the distributive and collective notions of power are compatible to the extent that, even if *a* has power over *b*, "the collective power of *a* and *b* [over *c*] is . . . enough for *b* to compensate for the disadvantages created by the subordinate position in the distributive power relation" (244). If this were characterized as a "trickle-down" theory of power, that would only serve to highlight Heiskala's point that both distributive and collective forms of power are based on a common conception of power as a kind of resource which, like wealth, can be given, taken, shared, increased or decreased, and so on.

Heiskala is at pains to identify the commonalities between distributive and collective approaches to power because they are widely regarded as competing and incommensurable views. Gordon (1980), for example, refers to

> two antithetical conceptions of power whose conjunction and disjunction determine the ground rules of most modern political thought: on the one hand, the benign sociological model of power as the agency of social cohesion and normality, serving to assure the conditions of existence and survival of the community, and on the other the more polemical representation of power as an instance of repression, violence and coercion.
>
> (Gordon 1980, 234–235)

Medical sociology was established in the Parsonian tradition, which approximates the first conception of power that Gordon describes in the preceding quote. The sick role (Parsons 1951) can be understood to involve a form of power that inheres in the relationship between individuals and medical professionals as both parties cooperatively pursue power over a manifestation of nature (i.e. ill health). It emphasizes power-*with* rather than power-*over*. As Jordens and Montgomery suggest in Chapter 2, however, with the declining influence of Functionalist sociology in the academy during the 1960s, collective notions of power were displaced by the notion of domination, which conforms more to the second model that Gordon describes. By the 1970s, in the sociological academy at least, notions of dominance came to dominate (so to speak), as exemplified by the work of Friedson (1970) in the United States and Willis (1991) in Australia.

According to Heiskala (2001) *structural* approaches to power conceive of power as a "network of relations" rather than as a resource, and they are exemplified by the work of Foucault. Whilst much can and has been said about the scope and influence of Foucault, Heiskala highlights one distinguishing feature which is particularly germane here, and that is the notion that power relations are "internal" rather than "external." This is to say that the identities of subjects (i.e. those who stand in relations of power) are not

> determined independently of and prior to the power relation, but rather . . . they represent a state of this network. . . . [I]n an internal relation between *a* and *b*, the identity of *a* depends on the identity of *b*. . . . [This] shifts the focus from the poles of the relation to the relation connecting these poles, which Foucault called . . . the *mechanism* of power. . . . Therefore, *a* and *b* are . . . related to each other in ways that do not simply make *b* subordinated and *a* free . . . [rather] the mechanism of power ties them to one another and is "transmitted . . . through them" by shaping the identity of each.
>
> (Heiskala 2001, 245–246)

During the 1980s, with the increasing influence of Foucauldian scholarship, notions of power that construe it as a resource (i.e. both collective and distributive notions of power) were displaced by structural notions, especially in humanities disciplines. Thus, two shifts occurred during the twentieth century regarding notions of power. Within medical sociology there was a shift away from a collective, Parsonian approach (a focus on power-*with*) towards something more like domination (power-*over*) and within the humanities there was a shift away from resource theories of power towards structural approaches. Both shifts had a bearing on what kind of power is understood to operate in and through the profession of medicine, and they explain the emergence of two distinct criticisms of medicine during the later decades of the twentieth century. It is to these criticisms that I will now turn.

Political Critiques of Medicine

The Critique of Medicalization

The term "medicalization" was coined in the early 1970s to account for the expansion of medicine into new domains. The literature on this topic is characterized by descriptive aims and also by concerns and anxieties about the consequences of what might be called "overreach." Such concerns are not new. Arguably, they stand at the origin of modernity. Shelley's (1969 [1818]) novel *Frankenstein*, for example, can be interpreted as a moral tale that expresses ambivalence about the medical applications of a new technology that we now call "electricity." By animating an assemblage of dead body parts with the spark of life, a medical scientist overreaches ("plays God"), and thereby unleashes his own punishment (nemesis). The novel's subtitle (*The Modern Prometheus*) links the tale to concerns about technology that stand at the origin of Western civilization.

More recent roots of the term can be traced to Szasz's critique of psychiatry. Szasz (1960), for example, characterizes the concept of mental illness as an extension of the medical concept of disease[2] to what he calls "problems of living." The latter, he argues, should be understood and treated as a normal part of human social life rather than as effects caused by the mental equivalent of a physical disease (i.e. they call for psychotherapy rather than medication).

What Szasz saw as a problem of classification and professional demarcation was later characterized by Zola (1972) as part of a much broader process in which medicine was displacing religion and law as the main institution of social control. Zola characterized this process as "medicalization." The question that concerns us here is what kind of power is seen to be at work in this process?

Zola observes that historically, medicine has clearly had recourse to familiar and coercive powers of law and state. These have been used in public health to enforce measures such as quarantine and in psychiatry to involuntarily confine people considered socially deviant. Zola's account of the social control exercised through medicine, however—*considered as a form of power in its own right*—is anomalous with respect to theories of power current at the time. His characterization of it is somewhat sketchy, but it is also prescient and it was clearly influential.

Zola describes a form of power that is exercised neither through overtly coercive means such as violence and confinement nor through "softer" mechanisms of collective power such as roles and shared values. It is exercised through expert judgement. Furthermore, it is expanding its remit or jurisdiction "beyond concern with ordinary organic disease" (494) to include other forms of social deviance such as addiction, normal phenomena such as pregnancy, ageing, and "problems of living," and the enhancement of human capabilities such as intelligence (495, 497). Its expansion is characterized by an increasing "extension into life" which is driven by efforts to prevent chronic diseases before they take hold and which is enabled by greater acceptance of certain "concepts" such as comprehensive medicine (e.g. White, Brown, and Wittkower 1954) and psychosomatics:

> It is no longer necessary for the patient merely to divulge the symptoms of his body, but also the symptoms of daily living, his habits and his

worries . . . it has become increasingly necessary to intervene to change permanently the habits of a patient's lifetime—be it of working, sleeping, playing or eating.

(Zola 1972, 493)

Notwithstanding its expansionist tendencies, Zola explicitly refuses to characterize this form of social control in the terms of political criticism that were current at the time, such as professional "imperialism" (487). He characterizes medicalization as "an insidious and often undramatic phenomenon" and stresses the interest and agency of society in this process:

This "medicalizing of society" is as much a result of medicine's potential as it is of society's wish for medicine to use that potential.

(Zola 1972, 500)

Medicalization leads not to an abject state of oppression or loss of autonomy but to "reluctant reliance on the expert." Despite its politically anodyne representation, this form of power is cast in a struggle that is as culturally significant as it is invisible:

The medical arena is the arena . . . par excellence of today's identity crisis—what is or will become of man. It is the battleground, not because there are visible threats or oppressors, but because they are almost invisible; not because the perspectives, tools or practitioners of medicine and the other helping professions are evil, but because they are not . . . here the technical danger is greater, for not only is the process masked as a technical, scientific, objective one, but one done for our own good.

(Zola 1972, 502)

The concept of medicalization soon took hold in critical writings, some of which struck a different political tone even if there were clear similarities in the concerns expressed. For example, Illich (1976) also argues that the increasing medicalization of life leads to greater reliance on professional expertise and that this has important cultural ramifications. Illich's terms are highly polemical, however, and the exercise of power is portrayed as unidirectional: health is "expropriated" *by* the medical profession, which leads to "disabling dependence" of the laity. Furthermore, this is only one adverse consequence of a process that unfolds between individuals in clinical interactions, at the level of organizations and institutions, and at a cultural level, with iatrogenic harms at each level amplifying each other in an irreversible, positive feedback loop. Drawing on the same mythic source as Shelley (1969 [1818]), Illich characterizes this outcome as a medical "nemesis," and thereby frames it as a *punishment* for medicine's "overreach" (34–35).

As Szasz's seminal work suggests, the concept of disease has featured prominently in the literature of medicalization. The general idea is that medicine brings new domains of human experience under its jurisdiction by recon-struing them as "something like a disease." This thesis plays an important role in Abbott's (1988) study of the professions as a social system that is constantly reconfigured by competition between professions for control over jurisdictions. Both collective and distributive notions of power are evi-dent in his account of inter-professional politics: normally, one profession's gain is another's loss, but professions sometimes maintain control over a jurisdiction through supervisory control of a subordinate profession that deals with routine work (25).[3] Abbott gives particular prominence to a form of symbolic control that he characterizes as "abstraction," however, and in the profession of medicine, the relevant abstraction is the concept of disease:

> Control of the occupation lies in control of the abstractions that gener-ate the practical techniques.
>
> (Abbott 1988, 8)

> It is with abstraction that American medicine claims all of deviance, the abstraction of its all-powerful disease metaphor.
>
> (Abbott 1988, 30)

In other words, the kind of power exercised by professions is to an impor-tant extent a form of symbolic power enabled by their knowledge systems. Knowledge increasingly features as something *internal* to the concept of power. This notion is also evident in subsequent efforts by Clarke et al. (2003) to account for the increasing influence of medicine on Western cul-ture in the latter half of the twentieth century.

Clarke et al. (2003) renovate the concept of medicalization to account for "dramatic changes in the organization and practices of biomedicine," and their explanation of the renovated concept of "biomedicalization" includes several claims that are relevant to the current discussion. First, what Zola characterized as "the extension into life" is no longer simply a greater intru-sion into social experience but a technological power to transform biologi-cal life itself. Second, because Clarke et al. (2003), like Abbott (1988), make knowledge integral to the kind of power exercised through medicine, they also seek to account for radical changes in the way that knowledge is pro-duced, distributed, and used. Chief among these changes is what we have come to call the information revolution, and this manifests in the health sector in different ways. One is the ubiquitous use of computers and data-banks to surveil, quantify, and analyze almost every aspect of our lives and use the resulting information to generate knowledge about how they relate to health and disease. Another manifestation is the expansion of the capi-talist economic system to and through the internet ("digital capitalism"). And a third manifestation is that non-experts are gaining greater access to this knowledge. The latter trend is worth noting in light of the authors' political aim "to allow greater democratic participation in shaping human futures *with* technosciences" (166) and also in light of Illich's (1976) image of a society utterly subjugated by professional imperialism. My point is that if (bio)medical knowledge is a form of power, it is no longer exclusively available to the medical profession. An important element of the power is increasingly at the disposal of the laity.

Notwithstanding attempts of Clarke et al. (2003) to renovate the concept of medicalization, its currency has endured. Its most comprehensive articulation is Conrad (2007), which elaborates medicalization in terms of its objects (*what* is medicalized), its agents (*who* does the medicalizing), the context of medicalization (i.e. factors which amplify or constrain medicalization), and the consequences of medicalization, which, as Parens (2013) argues, can be good or bad. Despite the apparent equanimity of recent scholarship, however, concerns about "overreach" persist. For example, the recent literature on "overdiagnosis" focuses concerns about the various ways in which medicine's diagnostic categories are (over)extended (see, e.g. Welch, Schwartz, and Woloshin 2011 and Carter et al. 2015). In other words, concerns about "overreach" still haunt the discourse of medicalization, like the ghost of Ivan Illich.

The Critique of Reductionism

The critique of medicalization emerged against the background of another persistent critique that takes medicine to task for its *reductionist* tendencies. Understood as a political criticism, the critique of reductionism turns on a different view of power—one that is more akin to what Heiskala (2001) characterizes as structural approaches to power. It is positive or productive. It frames power as "power-to" (capacity) rather than "power-over" (domination) or "power-with" (cooperation). It is often articulated using the metaphor of "internalization" and through well-worn scopic metaphors for knowledge.[4] For example, a form of power is seen to be at work when we "internalize" a particular world *view* or *perspective*. In a relationship of domination (to take a familiar version of the argument), one can "internalize" an ideology either as an oppressor or as the oppressed (the problem of false consciousness). This understanding of power was widely popularized in the new social movements of the 1960s and 1970s, particularly the civil rights movement and second wave feminism, for which power manifested not only as physical violence and coercion but in symbolic forms that left a lesion on human consciousness, as it were.

In the broadest form of this argument, the acquisition of knowledge is itself seen as the operation of a form of power. This extends the tendency identified earlier to see knowledge as something internal to power rather than as something separate.[5] It is a well-worn truism that knowledge *is* power in that it bestows certain capacities and enables possibilities that are constrained only by human imagination, but it can also be argued that, in acquiring knowledge, we also become subjects of power or discipline (i.e.

power of the self over the self). One of the ways in which this view departs from notions of domination is that autonomy can be understood as an outcome or effect of the exercise of power as much as something that power suppresses. Finally, this understanding of power is structural in the sense outlined earlier: the knower and the known are bound to each other by a mechanism of power that shapes the identity of each. As Heiskala (2001) suggests, this view of power is closely associated with the work of Foucault, and indeed, Foucault's notion of the medical gaze is an example of a scopic metaphor for medical knowledge. If it is understood as an effect on consciousness, it is not a lesion so much as a matrix through which the human body becomes available to consciousness (Foucault 1973 [1963]).[6]

At this point it will help to outline how the critique of reductionism typically proceeds. What concerns us here is how scientific reductionism in medicine enters the humanistic gaze—a gaze that is oriented to the epistemological and ethical effects of medicine as a field of human experience where life is brought under the scrutiny of scientific research and the influence of professional practice.

Where knowledge is characterized by scopic metaphors, it is usually implied (if not stated) that there are different ways of seeing the world, some of which are scientific. Furthermore, in humanistic criticism of medicine, scientific ways of seeing the world are commonly characterized using two tropes, namely, reductionism and narrowness. Broadly speaking, reductionism refers to a tendency to explain some "level" of reality with reference to causal relationships in what is understood to be a more basic or fundamental level of reality. The concept of disease "mechanisms" in the clinical sciences is an example of reductionism in this sense. The value of this kind of knowledge to medicine is that it reveals new points in a disease process to intervene in order to slow the process down, arrest it, or even reverse it.

If knowledge is understood as a relationship of power between the knower and the known, what are the effects on each in this epistemic environment? The knower "sees" the known with a narrowness of vision that reduces the known to a partial object. This effect can be characterized as negative in two senses. First, if one sees a thing partially, one's field of vision has been reduced (one has a negative epistemological scotoma, as it were). By the same token, if the object is partial, something is missing from it. Second, it is *better* to see things with broad vision than narrowly; it is *better* to see the whole than to see only a part. The first sense of negative is descriptive, and the second sense is normative.

The normative meaning motivates the need for remedial measures. Hence, the knower should be "cured" of narrow sight by being endowed with "broader" vision, and the known object should be rescued from reduction by being made whole in the eyes of the knower. Both cure of the knower and rescue of the known are vouchsafed by a different way of "seeing," one furnished by a humanities discipline or humanistic values. This anamorphic correction typically permits the widening of vision and expansion of objects in a particular direction or along a particular "vector." Finally, these vectors define the metaphorical space through which medicine expands into the lifeworld.

As we have seen, Zola (1972) characterized the expansion of medicine into new domains of life as a form of power or "social control." He also suggested that this expansion occurs along definable "vectors." In the following section, I will restate this argument, drawing on some philosophical distinctions to differentiate these vectors. This will help to trace the lines of tension between the critique of medicalization and the critique of reductionism into specific fields of practice where they manifest as new *ideologies of care* that compete against established ones.

"Vectors" of Medicine's Expansion

If we think of professional work as bringing expert knowledge to bear on problems of living, one vector of expansion is oriented to an epistemological question: what causes the problem? Another vector of expansion is oriented to an ontological question: who or what "has" the problem? And a third vector of expansion is oriented to an axiological question: what values are at stake? I will briefly consider each of these in turn.

The "Upstream" Vector: From the Effect to the Cause

Medicine is, among other things, a bulwark against threats to life and particularly diseases. Many diseases are easier to treat if they are detected at an early stage, which explains why the concept of disease shades into the concept of "pre-diseases" such as ductal carcinoma in situ (DCIS) and cervical dysplasia (in the case of malignant disease) and pre-diabetes and metabolic syndrome (in the case of chronic disease). Such entities test the classic naturalistic definition of disease (Boorse 1975), and they cast a wider epidemiological net. They are the targets of mass screening campaigns (e.g. for skin cancer and bowel cancer) and campaigns that aim to ensure early diagnosis (e.g. by encouraging self-examination of breasts or skin). The liminal concept of "pre-disease," in turn, shades into "risk factors" for disease such as hypertension, obesity, risky behaviours, and so on. These are also targets for screening, and they are targets for public health interventions that aim, as Zola (1972) put it, "to change permanently the habits of a patient's lifetime" (493). Risk factors, in turn, shade into social determinants of health such as public hygiene, the quality of housing, and social disadvantage.

The further one moves "upstream" along the vector of causal antecedents, two things happen. The first is that the concept of disease fades away as the direction of the medical gaze reverses. Instead of penetrating further and further into our biological reality (the body, the organ, the cell, the genome), it is projected outwards into our social world and bioecology. Second, the politics of medicine shade into the politics of city and state. This, of course, is no surprise to public health practitioners, who are often adept in the tasks of political advocacy, lobbying, policymaking, and even legislation. That said, it also entails that medical authority extends further and further into social life and government.

The stereotypical protest against expansion of social control along this vector is that it becomes "overweening": we are not dominated so much as smothered in the protective bosom of a "nanny state." Apart from the muffled protests of libertarians, however, such intrusions are widely tolerated. This is not only because they are done for our own good (Zola 1972) or because they are done in the name of humanistic values (e.g. for the health of the race, the nation, or humankind in general). It is because for millions of people they *actually do* most of the good.[7] Most of the health benefits that medicine generates are the outcomes of public health interventions (McKeown 1976). Furthermore, entities such as pre-diseases, risk factors, and social determinants of health are the abstractions of an *ideology of care* that no longer struggles to influence practice because it has been institutionalized as a specialty within medicine (i.e. preventive medicine or public health practice). From the point of view of the profession, the struggle is over; the jurisdictional frontier is peaceful (Abbott 1988). For libertarians, the horse has bolted.

The "Metaphorical" Vector: From the Part to the Whole Person

Synecdoche is a metaphor in which the part represents the whole (or vice versa).[8] A typical response to reductionism is to imagine a vector that links the part to the whole and then seek to widen the medical gaze so that the whole—or at least more of it—comes into view. This form of argument is a rich stalking ground for ideologies of care that aim to remediate what are thought to be the adverse effects of scientific reductionism in medicine.

Some of these ideologies have sought to extend the medical gaze beyond the body to mental life. This is the project of psychosomatic medicine, which gained enormous influence in the early twentieth century through Freudian psychology and which has maintained a following in the practice of psychotherapy. It also influenced ideologies of care that emerged mid-century, such as comprehensive medicine (White, Brown, and Wittkower 1954) and sought to integrate biological, psychodynamic, and sociological knowledge in both clinical practice and medical education. Comprehensive medicine was, in turn, a precursor to the biopsychosocial model of care (Engel 1977) which emerged in the 1970s and became widely taught in medical curricula. This model has been extended further to include a spiritual domain so that relationships with "transcendent" phenomena can also be factored in (Sulmasy 2002). By seeking to place "the whole person" or "the person behind the disease" centre stage (Steiger et al. 1960), comprehensive medicine also anticipated patient-centred care (see Chapter 2) and holistic care, which stands at one limit of this vector.

"Holistic" care does not foreclose on what aspects or dimensions of a person can become the object of therapeutic action. In general terms, if anything can be construed as an aspect of a person, then it legitimately comes under the purview of "holistic" care. If a person is conceived to have (for example) an astral body, or a virtual life, or multiple incarnations, all of these can become objects of expert judgement and authority. This vector of expansion thus brings medicine into competition with non-orthodox healing systems (Clouser and Hufford 1993). Drawing on Abbott's (1988) insight concerning abstractions, this can be explained by the fact that the concept of a person is an abstraction that is contested by many professions but controlled by none.

Although there is a striking continuity between the various ideologies of care that emerged during the second half of the twentieth century to counter the effects of reductionism, there are also differences that deserve a mention. One arises from the "narrative turn" in medical sociology, which enables the expansion of the medical gaze into subjective experience. This counters the "narrow" and reductionist tendencies of medicine in several novel ways. First, it legitimizes subjective experience as a domain of expert knowledge. Second, it counters the "reductionist" preference for causal, biological explanations by enabling explanations based on relations of signification: medical knowledge thereby becomes open to questions about meaning, culture, discourse, and identity. Third, the "narrative turn" helps to counter the narrowness of a gaze that is confined to institutionally defined "episodes" of care. This is particularly limiting in relation to chronic diseases: because the latter fundamentally disrupt everyday life, the full range of their effects can be understood only against the wider background of a patient's biography.

Many of these points were made in Kleinman's (1988) seminal book on illness narratives, which also outlines a humanistic ideology of care more suited to the chronic diseases of the twentieth century than the one his functionalist forebears had to offer. The main point to glean here is that the narrative turn brings the patient's subjectivity, values, cultural beliefs, identity, and everyday life within the purview of the medical gaze, along with their full personal history (as opposed to just their medical history). Indeed, if the ambition of holistic care is realized, no aspect of personhood is left concealed or off-limits. The expansion of medical jurisdiction along this vector is always justified in the name of a more humane ideology of care, but it is hard not to conclude that the more humane the care, the more comprehensive the gaze.

The "Value" Vector: From Negative to Positive Health

Medicine has often been criticized for being narrow—or perhaps lopsided—on the grounds that it focuses on diseases and deficits (subnormal function) to the neglect of "positive" attributes such as health, wellness, strength, vigour, resilience, and so on. This kind of criticism is famously enshrined in the WHO's definition of health (World Health Organization 1948). It emanates not from the humanities so much as from public health and health promotion in particular and also critical literature on disability (e.g. Amundson 2000). These are pockets of theory and practice that have provided a rich stalking ground for political advocacy and activism.

As Boorse (1977) argues, positive notions of health are normative through and through, so the pursuit of positive health means establishing healthy norms. As health authorities increasingly seek to intervene "upstream," furthermore, establishing "healthy" norms increasingly implicates everyday activities such as physical activity (what is the healthy minimum?), alcohol consumption (what is the healthy maximum?), sexual activity (how often is enough?), sleep and recreation (how much is enough?), and so on. Reorienting medicine to health and wellness thus helps to expand the domain in which norms can be defined by experts.

Along with the exhortation to holistic care, the push to establish "healthy" norms has become a feature of new age and other non-orthodox ideologies of care and particularly of the "wellness" movement. So both orthodox medicine and non-orthodox healing systems have expanded along both the "metaphorical" vector and the "value" vector, and the further medicine drifts away from its "all-powerful disease metaphor" (Abbott 1988), the more it finds itself involved in border skirmishes with the latter (see Figure 7.1).

Reflections on Political Criticism of Medicine and Ideologies of Care

One of the premises of this chapter is that medicine deals with questions of value not only by means of its own ethics (i.e. biomedical ethics, or bioethics) but also by means of its own politics. One of the aims of this chapter has been to describe these politics by focusing on what I take to be two of its manifestations: political criticism of medicine and what I call "ideologies of care." I will conclude with some brief reflections on each of these considerations.

Criticism of Criticism

Criticism is often characterized as a "negative" activity, which presumably means that it merely detracts from its target. When it comes to criticism of medicine, nothing could be further from the truth. Political criticism of medicine is productive. It stimulates change in medical practices that are spearheaded by ideologies of care, and in so doing it has helped to shape contemporary professions and institutions. Like the parasite, criticism is an exciter (Gullestad n.d.): it stimulates the expansion of medicine's jurisdiction into new domains of human life and experience and its intrusions into the jurisdictions of other professions (Abbott 1988).

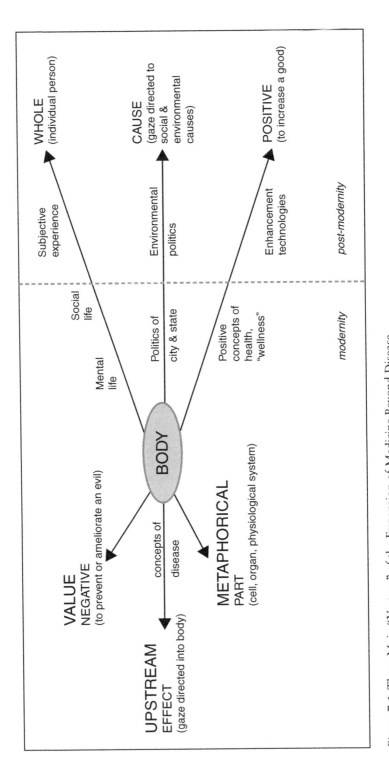

Figure 7.1 Three Main "Vectors" of the Expansion of Medicine Beyond Disease

The concept of disease is thought to play an important part in this process. The literature on medicalization and, more recently, the literature on disease mongering (e.g. Moynihan and Henry 2006) and over-diagnosis attest to this fact. But humanistic values are also a driver of medicine's expanding jurisdiction (Conrad 2007). This chapter fleshes out that claim. It also gives reasons to question the persistent focus on the concept of disease in the critical literature. As Zola stated more than forty-five years ago, medicine is increasingly characterized by efforts to shift *beyond* the concept of disease. It is expanding along vectors that are not limited by the naturalistic concept that Szasz (1960) and Boorse (1975) imagine. The more medicine strives to see the person behind the disease, the more the abstraction of disease gives way to the abstraction of a person, which no profession can or should control. The more medicine seeks to prevent disease by stemming its causes, the more the concept of disease is displaced by the abstractions of public health and social epidemiology. And the more medicine seeks to promote health and well-being, the more it occupies itself with concepts and phenomena other than disease.

From the point of view of medical politics, when medicine claims jurisdiction over a new or existing problem of living, the main question to ask is not whether that problem conforms to a positivist definition of disease distilled from medical theory by philosophical analysis (Boorse 1975). The main question is which kind of social control is preferable: that exercised by health professionals or that exercised by some other social group or authority? There is, of course, a third option: *no* social control. Zola's (1972) original reflections on social control suggest that this is open to us only to the extent that we are able to live outside of expert systems. This is the solution for which Ivan Illich advocated and for which he is often dismissed. It runs afoul of the Foucauldian maxim that there is no outside to power. If the Foucauldian maxim is true, then medicine *must* have its own politics.

I have differentiated two strands of criticism that are often invoked together. These criticisms are best understood in relation to each other and with due acknowledgement of the tension between them. One strand of criticism (the critique of reductionism) tends to propel medicine into new jurisdictions, whereas the other (the critique of medicalization) tends to hold it back, or impose limits (Illich 1976). It is in this respect that the politics of medicine are "elastic." These opposing forces can be understood as an expression of ambivalence about medical applications of scientific knowledge and new technologies—an ambivalence that was articulated with great imagination and artistry on the threshold of modernity (Shelley 1969 [1818]). The critique of medicalization encodes concerns and caution about "overreach." The critique of reductionism seeks to harness increasing social control—and, indeed, mastery of "life itself"—to humanistic values. But humanism also fuels the engines of modernity and postmodernity. We "play god" because in the human sciences there is no longer a god to hold us back or punish us.

Ideologies of Care and Their Discontents

What I call "ideologies of care" are often referred to as "models" of care or sometimes "paradigms." The word "models" is misleading, however, because models are usually representations of something that actually exists rather than something that *should* exist. "Model" can, of course, have a normative meaning. If you call someone a "model student," for example, you are holding him or her up as an exemplar. The word "model" is thus normatively ambiguous. I have used the term "ideology" because of its association with politics. I do not mean to imply that ideologies of care are a kind of false consciousness, however. I see them, rather, as a means of influencing medical practice with politically normative ideals that, from a philosophical point of view, implicate the use of causal knowledge, ontological questions, and questions about values.

The point about causal knowledge is that it should be used for prevention of disease. If this sounds obvious, that is because no-one nowadays cares to question it, and professions and institutions are in place to implement preventive measures and programmes. The ontological question asks *what* is it that health professionals apply their abstract knowledge to, if not disease? If this question is puzzling, it is because medicine itself gives many different answers (e.g. a disorder; a problem of living; a patient; a person; a population; a gene). Finally, regarding values, what is the goal of the medical profession's endeavours? Is it to prevent or ameliorate an evil (i.e. disease) or is it also to increase a good (e.g. health)? If this question sounds idle, it is not. As Boorse (1975) argues, in the case of disease, "all therapeutic programs converge on one goal," which is the absence of disease, whereas "positive health is not one ideal but a kind from which various ideals may be selected and pursued" (571). So if medicine also aims to increase positive health, it must contend with the political problem of pluralism because ideals of the good vary widely (and wildly). It follows that the more medicine expands along the "value" vector towards health, welfare, and beyond that, to enhancement of human being—and perhaps even to "post-human" being—the more important the theory and practice of value pluralism becomes. This, precisely, is where the final chapter of this book takes us.

Finally, ideologies of care show how medicine is *responsive* to criticism, but as the previous chapters of this book illustrate, this responsiveness redounds on the experience of healthcare professionals in ways that can trouble them. For example, ideologies of care can give rise to trouble where they seek to override the need for ethical judgement (see Chapter 2). They also trouble the experience of health professionals as they disrupt and compete with ways of "doing" care that have congealed into normal, accepted practice. Over their careers, health professionals probably have to deal with a succession of these ideologies, each of which has its advocates whose enthusiasm and impatience (and occasionally, no doubt, their zealotry and absolutism) demand a degree of tolerance. If an ideology of care manages to disrupt the current paradigm, it must be woven into the fabric of care (as discussed in Chapter 2). If it is truly successful, it eventually ossifies into a despised orthodoxy (as discussed in Chapter 3). This is a sign of its influence and success, and in all likelihood it also portends an impending "paradigm shift" in the theory and practice of care.

Notes

1. The fact it is enshrined in everyday usage suggests that the distributive notion of power is also the "common-sense" notion of power.
2. Szasz uses the terms "illness," but what he means by it corresponds to a naturalistic conception of disease, that is, deviation from the normal structural and functional integrity of the human body (Szasz 1960, 45).
3. An example here would be the relationship between medicine and nursing or specialized techniques of diagnostic imaging. See Abbott (1988, 71–72).
4. Scopic metaphors for knowledge such as "insight," "view," and "perspective" are so ubiquitous in English that it is hard to discuss knowledge without using them (they occur, for example, throughout this chapter). They can distract attention from language, however, which is a much more important consideration than visual perception when it comes to understanding what knowledge is. This is why Abbott's (1988) emphasis on abstraction is so useful.
5. The idea that knowledge and power are separate phenomena is captured in the dictum "the pen is mightier than the sword."
6. If we abandon the metaphor of the mind, the matrix can be understood as language and discourse.
7. It is important to keep in mind that under racialized political ideologies, medical authorities have also been implicated in great *harms* to millions of people (see, e.g. Breggin 1993). This motivates my later assertion that the concept of a person is an abstraction that no profession can *or should* control.
8. Referring to clothing as "threads" or (ironically) to a single soldier as "the army" are examples of synecdoche.

References

Abbott, A. 1988. *The system of professions: An essay on the division of expert labor.* Chicago, IL: University of Chicago Press.

Amundson, R. 2000. Against normal function. *Studies in History and Philosophy of Biological and Biomedical Sciences* 31(1): 33–53.

Boorse, C. 1975. On the distinction between disease and illness. *Philosophy and Public Affairs* 5: 49–68.

———. 1977. Health as a theoretical concept. *Philosophy of Science* 44(4): 542–573.

Breggin, P.R. 1993. Psychiatry's role in the holocaust. *International Journal of Risk and Safety in Medicine* 4(2): 133–148.

Carter, S., W. Rogers, C. Degeling, J. Douts, and A. Barratt. 2015. The challenge of overdiagnosis begins with its definition. *British Medical Journal* 350: h869.

Clarke, A.E., J.K. Shim, L. Mamo, J.R. Fosket, and J.R. Fishman. 2003. Biomedicalization: Technoscientific transformations of health, illness, and U.S. biomedicine. *American Sociological Review* 68(2): 161–194.

Clouser, K.D., and D.J. Hufford. 1993. Nonorthodox healing systems and their knowledge claims. *Journal of Medicine and Philosophy* 18(2): 101–106.

Conrad, P. 2007. *The medicalization of society: On the transformation of human conditions into treatable disorders.* Baltimore, MD: Johns Hopkins University Press.

Engel, G. 1977. The need for a new medical model: A challenge for biomedicine. *Science* 196(4286): 129–136.

Friedson, E. 1970. *Professional dominance: The social structure of medical care.* New York, NY: Atherton Press.

Foucault, M. 1973 [1963]. *The birth of the clinic: An archaeology of medical perception.* London: Tavistock.

Gordon, C. 1980. Afterword. In *Power/knowledge: Selected interviews and other writings 1972–77 by Michel Foucault,* edited by C. Gordon, 229–259. Sussex: Harvester Press.

Gullestad, A.M. n.d. Parasite. In *Political concepts: A critical lexicon.* www.political concepts.org/issue1/2012-parasite/. Accessed April 26, 2018.

Heiskala, R. 2001. Theorizing power: Weber, Parsons, Foucault and neostructuralism. *Theory and Methods* 40(2): 241–264.

Illich, I. 1976. *Limits to medicine: Medical Nemesis: The expropriation of health.* London: Calder & Boyars.

Kleinman, A. 1988. *The illness narratives: Suffering, healing and the human condition.* New York, NY: BasicBooks.

McKeown, T. 1976. *The role of medicine: Dream, mirage or nemesis?* London: Nuffield Provincial Hospitals Trust.

Moynihan, R., and D. Henry. 2006. The fight against disease mongering: Generating knowledge for action. *PLoS Medicine* 3(4): e191.

Parens, E. 2013. On good and bad forms of medicalization. *Bioethics* 27(1): 28–35.

Parsons, T. 1951. Illness and the role of the physicians: A sociological perspective. *American Journal of Psychiatry* 21(3): 452–460.

Shelley, M.W. 1969 [1818]. *Frankenstein or the modern Prometheus.* Edited with an Introduction by M.K. Joseph. London: Oxford University Press.

Steiger, W.A., F.H. Hoffman, A.V. Hansen, and H. Niebuhr. 1960. A definition of comprehensive medicine. *Journal of Health and Human Behaviour* 1(2): 83–86.

Sulmasy, D.P. 2002. A biopsychosocial-spiritual model for the care of patients at the end of life. *The Gerontologist* 42(S3): 24–33.

Szasz, T. 1960. The myth of mental illness. *The American Psychologist* 15(2): 113–118.

Weber, M. 1978 [1922]. *Economy and society: An outline of interpretative sociology.* Edited by G. Roth and C. Wittich. Los Angeles, CA and London: University of California Press.

Welch, H.G., L.M. Schwartz, and S. Woloshin. 2011. *Overdiagnosed: Making people sick in the pursuit of health.* Boston, MA: Beacon Press.

White, K.L., J.S. Brown, and E.D. Wittkower. 1954. Comprehensive medicine. *The Canadian Medical Association Journal* 70(2): 115–122.

Willis, E. 1991. *Medical dominance: Division of labour in Australian health care.* Sydney: Allen & Unwin.

World Health Organization. 1948. *Constitution.* www.searo.who.int/about/about_searo_const.pdf. Accessed May 08, 2018.

Zola, I.K. 1972. Medicine as an institution of social control. *The Sociological Review* 20(4): 487–504.

8 Value Pluralism—The Bare Bones

Miles Little

Introduction

The chapters in this book cover diverse perceptions of quandaries faced by doctors and healthcare workers generally as they go about their daily business. Like everyone else, they have duties and interests that commonly cause countervailing tensions. Usually, these tensions are not of their own making but, as it were, come with the territory. If you care for individual patients, your attention to their individual needs necessarily exists within social contexts. What may seem best in a therapeutic sense may not be even practicable financially or may not even be available in a particular society or culture. The manufacturers and distributors of medications and medical technology hold vast funds and vast power, and somehow the healthcare workers must balance their own roles as supplicants to funders and suppliers and providers to the vulnerable. Money and power and status and vulnerability together make a confusing moral and practical mélange. Doctors and their healthcare colleagues must somehow make sense of the resulting complexity, making their way through murky paths of uncertainty and risk. They are inevitably troubled by ethics, self-interests, institutional expectations, legal and financial constraints, and personal involvements. It is hardly surprising that a book on quandaries should come into being. Each chapter examines perceptions of what it is to face quandaries in healthcare practice and research, and the whole book covers a selected few of the innumerable daily tensions encountered by healthcare workers.

Jordens and Montgomery in Chapter 2 tackle the tensions generated by systemic expectations of patient autonomy and informed consent. They accept the ethical importance of these categories but stress that expectations cannot be fully satisfied because of linguistic limitations and the paradox of autonomy. Language cannot fully evoke the experiences of treatments so severe that they threaten life in an attempt to prolong life. The paradox of autonomy may be expressed by refusal to listen to information, by refusal of treatment, or by voluntary rejection of selective parts of warnings and explanations given as part of education programmes. Such decisions are within the rights of patients but give rise to "blame games" and to potential frustration for all parties to the healthcare engagement. Everyone in the context of "extreme" medical treatment, doctors included, are subject to quandaries and to clashes between their duties, hopes, expectations, and experiences. Jordens and Montgomery encapsulate the experienced situation when they write:

> The upshot is that in BMT [Bone Marrow Transplantation], patients come to understand important facts, such as the onerousness of high dose chemotherapy, in the main retrospectively. This is frustrating for professionals who are heavily invested in rational systems. Perhaps they can take comfort in the thought that this is no different in other spheres of life. As a philosophical truism puts it, life is lived forwards in time but understood backwards.
>
> (this volume, 23)

The Lipworth and Montgomery chapter (Chapter 5) concerns the essentially contested concept involved in the tension between the business of pharma and the practice of medicine. It uses both empirical data from interviews and from publications on both sides of the essentially contested divide. It is oriented towards value pluralism (VP) because, in its first part, it deconstructs arguments from both sides and, in the second, extends the discourse by examining empirical data from interviews with people who work at research and management levels with Australian pharmaceutical companies. Both sections of the chapter invite us to examine the rhetoric and eristic employed by opposing sides and to appreciate the self-image of those who actually work for major pharmaceutical companies. In the manner of any VP analysis, it leads to no determinate conclusion but opens gateways of perception that provide nuanced insights into the claims of opposing sides, both of whom can agree on the common aims of healthcare, the benefits of research and innovation, and the need for ample funding for research and development but who disagree on moral and epistemological grounds.

Narcyz Ghinea and colleagues' contribution (Chapter 3) is about off-label prescribing and reasonableness. It looks into the breadth of what counts as "evidence," and it deals frankly with the practical fact that practice and experimentation merge into one another, despite the nicety of words used to separate them for ethical and political reasons. Ghinea and colleagues remind us that accountability for reasonableness (a disputed but convenient term which has been much discussed [Daniels 2000; Daniels and Sabin 2008; Martin, Giacomini, and Singer 2002; Carter and Little 2008]) is important when practice and policymaking are so much affected by changing contexts. To quote from their chapter,

> In his book *Return to Reason* (Toulmin 2009), the late British philosopher Stephen Toulmin astutely observed:

Intellectuals in the year 2000 . . . have inherited a family of problems about the idea of Rationality and its relations to those of necessity and certainty. But they tend to ignore the more practical, complementary idea of Reasonableness, or the possibility of living . . . without any absolute necessities or certainties.

Jessica Pace and colleagues' contribution (Chapter 4) is about the conflict inherent in the clinician's position between serving the individual patient and serving the public good. They contrast evidence provided by the passions (cf. Hume 1991) and cold, hard evidence with a numerical base and between the virtues of hope and compassion and the pragmatic demands of budgets. They also include empirical evidence and literature supporting the claim that a pluralist approach works only within the bounds of reasonableness.

Siun Gallagher's contribution (Chapter 6), by contrast, examines the perceptions of doctors who become expert advisors to resource allocating bodies. These professionals are experts by virtue of their medical training but relative outsiders amongst bureaucrats, policymakers, and economists. Their quandary is to secure a valid identity within this dual role, to remain clinicians with obligations to serve individual patients, while also serving public interests with limited resources. Medical training does not include a great deal about the formalities and realities of macroallocation.

Christopher Jordens's chapter (Chapter 7) takes a broad perspective of implicit quandaries raised for clinicians by competing critiques of their "political" positions. Medicine is practised under the gaze of politics (including economics), sociology, and philosophy. Its performances and its disasters are quickly made public by the media. This constant attention constitutes yet another quandary, a moral and practical uncertainty of choice and commitment. Jordens writes:

I want to suggest that the politics of medicine exist alongside the ethics of medicine as an important—if perhaps less well theorized—means by which medicine deals with questions of value.

(this volume, 107)

and again that,

the politics of medicine shade into the politics of city and state.

(this volume, 116)

Jordens unpacks the tensions between two different political and sociological critiques of medicine. He condenses the essence of these critiques as follows:

One calls medicine to account for its expansionist tendencies. In essence, this criticism is based on concerns about medicine "overreaching." Such

concerns are as old as modernity and perhaps as old as Western civilization itself, but they have found expression in recent decades, particularly
in the social sciences, as the *critique of medicalization*. The other line of
criticism calls medicine to account for its reductionist tendencies. This
critique is based on concerns about the effect of scientific knowledge on
both the knower and the known, and it has been cultivated particularly,
but by no means exclusively, in the humanities.

(this volume, 107–108)

All these diverse reflective and empirical chapters share one common
stance—that of a value pluralism (Galston 1999; Little et al. 2007; Rescher
1992; Tetlock 1986; Walzer 1995) that adopts a unifying view of engagement with and interrogation of the values that underpin the phenomena
of disagreement and quandary. Each seeks to establish some understanding of the premises and propositions from which opponents and interested
agents argue with one another and to indicate the—sometimes conflicting—
conclusions for ethics and policy that may be drawn from what are sup-
posed to be fair or pragmatic outcomes. This is a book informed by value
pluralism, and it is fair that we should examine its processes, aims, strengths,
and weaknesses.

So What Is Value Pluralism?

Value pluralism (VP) is a mode of discourse, a politic way to engage with
moral, epistemological, ontological, and political differences (Audi 2004;
Engelhardt 2011; Galston 1999, 2002; Rescher 1992; Tetlock 1986). In formal terms, its pluralism can be foundational, normative, or agentic. Agentic
pluralism offers insights, because it acknowledges the phenomena of individual difference but is not considered further because it is a manifestation
of implicit or explicit commitment to value pluralism as a practical way
to engage with the world and with other people's beliefs and judgements.
Gallagher's chapter emphasizes that agentic conflicts can be reconciled by a
process of discourse—but that discourse must be guided by some acceptance
of pluralism.

Pluralism and monism in foundations and norms are porous concepts and
bleed into one another. The foundational pluralism implied by support for
private enterprise, free speech, and same sex marriage as individual rights,
for example, can be brought together with other diverse commitments
under the (quasi-)monistic category of libertarianism (Loughlin 2014). Normative pluralism seeks ways to reconcile different societal norms under the
restraint of preserving safe and harmonious societies. Social tolerance of
differences in sexual orientation (when that actually happens) provides an
example of normative pluralism in action. In this book, Jessica Pace and colleagues write about the importance of the VP perspective in attempting to
achieve "an appropriate balance between thinking about the sustainability

of the healthcare system overall and ensuring that individual patient needs are met" (this volume, 56).

Value pluralism implies politeness to preserve discourse, tolerance to remain inclusive, scepticism to maintain openness to persuasion, and rule delimitation to define the extent to which tolerance can be pushed short of extreme relativism (Feyerabend 1993), which it does not support (Galston 1999, 2002; Gray 1978, 2016; Tetlock 1986). *It can exist only within frameworks of governance that delineate boundaries of liberty*—witness the failures of utopian social experiments (Holloway 1966) compared with the relative success of Quakerism.[1] Its domains are ontological, epistemological, ethical, and political, and its ecosystem is complexity. Like Stoicism or Epicureanism, it offers a philosophical standpoint of engagement with and assessment of the world. One of its central aims is to generate "discourse about discourse"—a process of informed and constructive critique of dominant ways of justifying claims.

To be taken seriously, value pluralism requires the resolution of three contested issues:

1   Can we make value pluralism a norm, when it requires scepticism toward norms and continued openness to the expressions of other values—a paradox that resembles the Euthyphro problem?
2   What criteria are appropriate for valid arguments so that loose relativism is avoided?
3   How should value pluralists approach definitions of truth criteria that might sustain valid arguments under a pluralist epistemology?

Because value pluralism suggests the benefits of contextual resolution of contested concepts and claims, it encourages dialectic and reflection. *Both are essential to its ontology, epistemology, ethics, and politics.* There are established disciplines and literatures on which it can draw. It is eclectic in its sources. Ethically, for example, its model is a form of radical reflective equilibrium (Daniels 1980, 1996; DePaul 1993 [2001]).[2] Ontological and epistemological models might be critical realism[3] (Archer et al. 1998; Bhaskar 1998) or foundherentism[4] (Haack 1993). Politically, it is claimed by certain thinkers in the liberal tradition (Galston 1999, 2002; Gray 1978; Kymlicka 1989). If it is to have a methodology, it would resemble a combination of appreciative inquiry and generative editing[5] (Bushe 2013; Gabler, Bornstein, and Pierce 1995). It has a central commitment to accountability to reasonableness (Daniels 2000; Daniels and Sabin 2008).

Value Pluralism, Liberalism, and Argument

There are, however, problems in associating liberalism too closely with the ethical commitments of value pluralism. The liberal tradition, and its neoliberal descendants, place reliance on a particular view of autonomy, whereby the autonomous individual has an atomistic status, a self-governing, self-directing, and self-responsible core. Individualism is a major tenet of liberal and neoliberal politics. Value pluralism respects individuals but also places them firmly within networks of social interconnection and support. An individual bears the consequences of family, education, friendships, faith, beliefs, and intuitions and expresses them in ways determined by genetic and epigenetic attributes, such as physical prowess, intelligence, and the chances of environment. Value pluralism sees autonomy as *relational* (Christman 2004; MacKenzie and Stoljar 2000) rather than atomistic, and therefore seeks to engage with the social background to contested concepts, rather than seeing ideologies as purely individual choices. This does not, again, reduce to a loose relativism, because the evolutionary, social, and moral arguments against some commitments—destructive ideologies such as Nazism or Stalinism—are convincing. Ideologies that seek to subvert functioning social order are eventually self-destructive. The French Revolution destroyed itself by creating an anarchy that produced a dictator as its outcome and its way back to some kind of order. Napoleon's order was enlightened in many respects but eventually self-destructive again because of its aspirations towards empire, control, and conquest, towards a hegemony that served the interests of a restricted group of people.

Value pluralism relies heavily on the emergence that comes from appreciative inquiry and generative editing (Bushe 2013; Gabler, Bornstein, and Pierce 1995). In the Aristotelian tradition (Aristotle 1976), it indicates that ethics concerns how a person should behave by suggesting that decisions about behaviour should emerge from sceptical and reflective engagement with other arguments. Lipworth and Montgomery illustrate that process as they deconstruct the contested practices of interaction between healthcare and the pharmaceutical industry in Chapter 5. Principles (Beauchamp and Childress 2001) and axioms (Daniels 1996; DePaul 1993 [2001]; Archer et al. 1998) and maxims (Grice 1975; Hogan and Schwartz 1984; Pound 1921)[6] provide each community with condensed ways to enunciate implicit values. They are useful insofar as they guarantee respectful evaluation of apparently conflicting conclusions about ways to behave (Cheung, Leung, and Au 2006; Hui, Bond, and Ng 2006; Joshanloo, Afshari, and Rastegar 2010; Bond et al. 2004; Hui et al. 2010; Kurman and Ronen-Eilon 2004; Lai, Bond, and Hui 2007; Leung et al. 2002). "Sincerity" is not a criterion for respect or acquiescence (Markovits 2006), for many reasons—partly because motives are inaccessible, partly because an arguer can sincerely believe in Nazism or opportunism or the superiority of a particular group and may, therefore, advocate oppression or the exploitation of vulnerability, contravening the VP commitment to the protection of negative liberties.

Value pluralism relies on argument, the genuine engagement between moderate partisans who represent opposing modes of expressing values (Galston 1999, 2002; Toulmin 1972; Walton 1996, 2006, 1989). It is not so much the foundational values expressed by principles that are likely to be in conflict as the beliefs that sustain the appropriate way to instantiate and deploy values—the axioms and maxims that arguers use to warrant their claims and counterclaims. There may be, for example, widespread agreement that is good for people to survive, be secure, and flourish, but neoliberals and socialists are unlikely to agree on many things—the criteria for flourishing and security, the groups entitled to flourish, the locus of responsibility for social welfare, the atomistic nature of the individual as against her social identity, and so on. Argument, however, breaks down when ideology rules out hearing and engaging with other beliefs and reasons. Ideology at its worst turns the receiver off and the transmitter on (Gee 1990; Geertz 1964; O'Neill 1987; Tauber and Sarkar 1993). Argument is replaced by debate, by attempts to correct the opposition, to establish the supremacy of one set of beliefs over another without taking on board whatever may be worth hearing from the other perspective (Ehninger 1970). Arguers resort to eristic and informal logical fallacies when they must try to shore up their ideological stances. Lipworth and Montgomery, for example, quote from an academic article dismissing the case that defends the place of pharmaceutical industry in research and healthcare with these words:

> Pharmaceutical company money, and the purchase of influence, has been the single most powerful distorting force in healthcare in a generation—this is undisputed.
>
> (Stone 2015, ¶5)

and again

> One thing here is true—no, we don't have prospective randomized trials showing that conflict of interest policies improve patient outcomes. But, such a stance is absurd.
>
> (Prasad 2015, ¶6)

The key words here are "undisputed" and "absurd." It is precisely financial COI and its possible baleful effects that is in dispute, and there is no self-contradiction, no absurdity, in proposing trials that might search for possible harmful effects of COI *in practice*. The first quote propagates an informal logical error by a form of *ignoratio elenchi*, by rejecting any counter-argument out of hand, by denying the validity of any opposing view. The second does something similar by drawing a universal conclusion despite there being no evidence to support "absurdity." Each author *may* have a valid point to make, but adversarial claims to unsupported authority remain unsupported. Scepticism and moral reflection need to be applied to both sides of the argument about the influences—good, bad, or neither—of the pharmaceutical industry on healthcare.

Lipworth and Montgomery's material also shows that Rosenbaum, who argued that there was much to commend the alliance between pharma and medicine, resorted to important assertions without quoting evidence or acceptable authority:

> As the public observes this spiral of blame and shame, the conflict-of-interest movement has paradoxically achieved what it set out to avert: an erosion of public trust in medicine and science.
>
> (Rosenbaum 2015, 2067)

There *may* have been erosion in public trust, but by what measures, made by whom? This is a sweeping claim that, for the VP practitioner, demands justification, because it is neither self-evident, nor necessarily axiomatic for all countries. There has been work on this matter that suggests a sharp decline in trust in the *leadership* of medicine and in the medical *system* in the United States but reasonable persistence of trust in individual doctors. Perceptions differed sharply between countries (Blendon, Benson, and Hero 2014). The conflict summarized in Lipworth and Montgomery's chapter bears the hallmarks of the anger, aggression, and eristic generated by an essentially contested concept (Gallie 1955). Adversarial language and polemic are unlikely to lead to any resolution, which would demand discipline, scepticism, reflection, and genuine engagement with the arguments of the opponents.

Scepticism, Reflection, and Moderate Partisanship

Value pluralism suggests (or requires) scepticism and reflection but depends on restrained partisanship in argument (Ehninger 1970). Moderate partisanship implies some kind of established cognitive, moral, or political "commitments" to act as reference points for the "validity" of arguments. Value pluralism can work only if practised within established frameworks, be they epistemological, moral, social, or political. Jessica Pace and colleagues in their chapter record the perspective of one of their interviewees, acknowledging the need for structure within which to function as a moral agent:

> The government have to set a condition about cost benefits, and you cannot argue that it doesn't matter if it works or not, it gives the patient hope. I think if you gave me $140,000 I could give hope to patients in all sorts of different ways, and I can do it for a lot less money.
>
> (this volume, 56)

Lipworth and Montgomery also quote from one of the interviewees in their study in a similar vein:

> We . . . need to be monitored. So while there is commercial gain in anything, you need to have a really good monitoring process in place. Individuals, people will be people. Adam Smith is right, so I guess we'd

be Wall Street. You need to have constant safeguards, either internally applied or sanctions externally applied, you can't just let go.

(this volume, 77)

Meanwhile, Jordens and Montgomery, from a different perspective agree when they claim:

The possibility of shared decision-making exists within limits that are exposed from time to time in the context of high-risk medical procedures. These limits are the points at which the parties to clinical decisions can exercise their autonomy by making *unilateral* decisions.

(this volume, 24)

Can VP, therefore, be dismissed because it must acknowledge its own lack of secular moral authority to compel compliance? The same weakness affects all moral systems, such as consequentialism or deontology, virtue ethics or principlism. All can indicate ways to think about moral quandaries and suggest morally reflective ways in which to act. But none can garner the force of law, and the coercive nature of the law trumps other concepts where widely acknowledged harms such as theft, rape, or murder are concerned (Breen, Plueckhahn, and Cordner 1997; Hart 1977; Kerridge, Lowe, and McPhee 2005). Legal punishment and sanctions have more power in civil societies where church condemnation has lost much of its power to threaten eternal punishment. Substantive punishment and shame in the present have largely usurped the threat of eternal suffering in many Western societies. Value pluralism suggests ways in which to evaluate the institutional logics (Thornton and Ocasio 1999; Thornton, Ocasio, and Lounsbury 2012) (or lack of them) that are expressed in judgements about "wrongdoing" and the adoption of social and legal norms. It asks that its adherents refine their discourse and their critical faculties while enhancing their own capacities as facilitators and mediators.

Value pluralism has to start from a position of some agreements on the values attached to human living, to security in that living, and to the opportunity to flourish in human ways (Little et al. 2012; Loughlin 2014). The big questions that then arise concern definitions of each foundational value and the search for reference points. Should equal respect be afforded to those who seek to disrupt the prevailing social order? Whose social order should predominate? Can local cultural ideas about social order and flourishing be respected if they infringe more widely accepted views of human rights? Can ideologies evolved in countries with moderate populations be used to evaluate fairly the governance evolved in counties with huge populations? How far can we stretch universalism in ethical and political thinking? We can stretch it further in the domain of epistemology. Even there, however, there can be widespread agreement about the facts of science but serious disagreements about the social or ethical interpretation of the facts. Climate change provides one obvious example of dissonance between measurements and interpretation (Hulme 2009; Weart 2003).

Value Pluralism as a Heuristic

Value pluralism is not a normative theory in the usual sense. It is a heuristic that suggests ways in which to proceed under conditions of conflict and disagreement within some ordering framework. It does not guarantee that its end-points will be either "right" or the "best forever." It suggests (at best) that they may work for the moment. Value pluralism could be no more successful in changing human nature than any other scientific, ethical, or political system (Blackburn 2014; Pinker 2002; Gray 1978). It offers only a way to proceed with maximal consideration of empirically, culturally, psychologically, and ethically relevant differences and commonalities. It is thus pragmatic (Dewey 1941; Morgan 2007; Rorty 1982; Toulmin 2009) in orientation, and it recommends dialectic (Low 1997) as a means to find justice (Walzer 1995) and reject false logic, unsubstantiated claims, ideologies that claim normative justification for the abolition of negative freedoms (Berlin 1969 [1958]), and ideologies that justify hegemonic control over harmless difference in thought, worship, association, or speech just because they are different (Galston 1999, 2002; Tetlock 1986). In short, it is an advisory, a set of moral and intellectual guidelines that suggests ways to reach joint decisions and seeks to minimize informal logical errors, draws contextually on both currently endorsed foundational and normative values, while encouraging informed and critical reflection and reflective scepticism and equilibrium (Daniels 1980, 1996; DePaul 1993 [2001]). It is a process of engagement with aims that are less ambitious than those sought by Habermas from his stricter structures of discourse (Habermas 1991). Its end-point is acquiescence rather than consensus (Rescher 1992). Its measures of success are temporary acceptance, pragmatic adoption, and sufficient public endorsement to ensure stability until contextual changes raise new challenges. Toulmin commended pragmatism by writing that it "is an honest foundation for knowledge, and avoids the specious claim that only abstract, self-validating Theory gives us genuine Certainty" (Toulmin 2009, 174). The pragmatic and heuristic components of decisions are made explicit by one of the interviewees recorded by Pace and colleagues:

> So while it's perfectly OK to talk about patient impact, and it's perfectly OK to have different input, you do need a rigorous non-emotional system that is able to say no, and that can withstand the emotional pleas. Because otherwise we'll bankrupt the country.
>
> (this volume, 58)

There have, of course, been many attempts to formulate rules for argument in the face of essentially conflicted concepts[7] (Gallie 1955). Habermas's discourse rules (Habermas 1992) are formal and demanding, no doubt effective if all parties agree to strict conformity with precepts that govern sincerity, turn-taking, consistency—from which Habermas felt that a result would emerge from the unforced force of the better argument. Because negotiations inevitably take place between imperfect and adversarial human beings, the Habermasian rules are unenforceable on unwilling discussants. Negotiation that accepts the desirability of interchange and the aim of mutual benefit has become a more realistic point of reference—although it still depends on the preparedness of the arguers to listen to one another.

Three processes can be mentioned, each suggesting that resolution *may* be achieved by following certain steps and each insisting on the value of third-party facilitation.

Kantrowitz (1977) and Mazur (1993) in the 1970s proposed a *"science court"* as a means of deciding the outcomes of scientific disputes, such as those arising from concerns about the health effects of high-tension power lines. The process is described in Kantrowitz's words:

> The basic mechanism proposed here is an adversary hearing, open to the public, governed by a disinterested referee, in which expert proponents of the opposing scientific positions argue their cases before a panel of scientist/judges. The judges themselves will be established experts in areas adjacent to the dispute. They will not be drawn from researchers working in the area of dispute, nor will they include anyone with an organizational affiliation or personal bias that would clearly predispose him or her toward one side or the other. After the evidence has been presented, questioned, and defended, the panel of judges will prepare a report on the dispute, noting points on which the advocates agree and reaching judgments on disputed statements of fact. They may also suggest specific research projects to clarify points that remain unsettled.
>
> (Kantrowitz 1977, 333)

The concept of a science court was opposed by scientists, who feared that such a "court" might become authoritarian. Writing in the 1990s, Mazur (1993) concluded:

> *There is no need for a panel of judges* to decide which adversary is correct because, most likely, neither adversary will be clearly correct. If I were reformulating the science court proposal today, I would leave out the judges, making it in effect a mediation process. This ought to satisfy critics who fear that the court would become authoritarian.
>
> (Mazur 1993, 168)

A few science courts were tried, but the idea (perhaps unfortunately) has gained little traction.

Ronald Fisher has developed and used *interactive conflict resolution* that involves analysis of the contested issue and identification of sticking points, confrontation with the contested issues to allow mutual acknowledgement of their nature, and resolution guided by a mutually agreed facilitator. Fisher points to successes in negotiations between the ethnic parties in Cyprus, between native and non-native interests in Canada, and progress towards negotiated settlement between Maori and Pakeha communities in New Zealand (further details of both the principles and practice of interactive conflict resolution can be found in Fisher 2016).

The other process that has attracted considerable attention emanates from Harvard. *Principled negotiation* involves similar stepwise phases of inquiry and discourse. It has five principles (Mandell, Keast, and Chamberlain 2017):

1   "Separate the people from the problem"
2   "Focus on interests, not positions"
3   "Invent options for mutual gain"
4   "Insist on using objective criteria"
5   "Know your BATNA (Best Alternative To Negotiated Agreement)."

Principled negotiation seems to find its main application in planned negotiations at management level and in the analysis of prominent cases of failure in dispute resolution (examples of its application to planned negotiations can be found in Mandell, Keast, and Chamberlain 2017).

These (and many other) approaches undoubtedly provide potentially helpful and potentially successful frameworks for negotiating settlements between parties in conflicts if and only if the opponents are willing to adopt bargaining positions that allow modification of their initial interests. The general thrust of these ideal processes urges a search for "win–win" outcomes, in which each party finds some gain that at least balances any apparent loss. There appears to be no prescribed process that will overcome insistence on unilateral "winning," nor is there any apparent way to change commitment to an ideological foundationalism, rather than one grounded in acknowledgement of evolution and the profundities and subtleties of "fitness" to survive and flourish. As Toulmin writes, the best deployment of the different forms of knowledge that can be brought to bear in examining quandaries requires that we adopt an attitude that

> brings into focus the relation of Ethical Theory to Moral Practice, which comes onto center stage at this point: the central issue is not the timeless question, "What general principles can be relied on to decide this case, in terms that are binding on everyone who considers it?" but rather the timely question, "Whose interests can be accepted as morally overriding in the situation that faces us here and now?"
>
> (Toulmin 2009, 122)

Gallagher's chapter in this volume examines the ways in which doctors handle the tensions inherent in being expert advisers faced with responsibilities to individual patients or patient groups and responsibilities to committees that deal with macroallocations. Her interviewees seem, by and large, to have accepted that dual agency quandaries could to a significant extent be managed by accepting the validity of the discursive *process* in which decisions were made, processes which demanded careful and balanced attention to "the interests that can be accepted as morally overriding in the situation that faces us here and now" (Toulmin 2009, 122):

> Even if it's not an outcome I agree with, if the process is fair then I'm happy with that.

> (this volume, 96)

Inherent Weaknesses

The serious weakness of value pluralism is its inability to influence value monists who derive their premises from concepts of power or money or hegemony or divine right, or any other monistic ideologies. There are no compelling reasons that can persuade the self- or group-interested to be otherwise than they are, because they have a vested interest in repelling welfare or evolutionary arguments by citing their own welfare and the welfare of their particular group. There is no secular moral authority that can enforce reflective conclusions (Engelhardt 2011). Human rights are fragile and can be abolished by "executive order" (Kennedy 2013). In the short term, autocracies may be more appropriate and successful than some democracies in creating stability for a time (e.g. the rule of Napoleon I). Populations may be too large and too diverse for polite dialectic, and periods of instability and disadvantage open the way to populists and strong-men. The "epistemology of ignorance" that is promoted during debates about race, for instance, makes ignorance a dynamic space in which to develop eristically persuasive arguments among those who refuse to consider alternative perspectives. In a book on the epistemology of ignorance, edited by Sullivan and Tuana, Charles Mills introduces his chapter with the following words:

> Imagine an ignorance that resists. Imagine an ignorance that fights back. Imagine an ignorance militant, aggressive, not to be intimidated, an ignorance that is active, dynamic, that refuses to go quietly—not at all confined to the illiterate and uneducated but propagated at the highest levels of the land, indeed presenting itself unblushingly as knowledge.

> (Mills 2007, 13)

Imagine, if you can, a better introduction to the post-truth era. Value pluralism may seem to be one possible antidote, but it cannot be made compulsory.

And So . . .

Value pluralism is, therefore, best conceived as a heuristic, a description of a reasonable way to proceed as contemporary humankind struggles to cope with the massive problems that are very largely of its own making, particularly since the so-called Great Acceleration from about 1950 onward (Gray 2016; Steffen et al. 2015). Social and political pluralisms are (precariously) entrenched as ideals in Western liberal societies. As Jordens argues, the conflicting demands that emerge from the critiques of medicine's expansionism and its reductionism mean that, among other things,

> if medicine also aims to increase positive health, it must contend with the political problem of pluralism because ideals of the good vary widely (and wildly).
>
> (this volume, 122)

It may well be, therefore, that we're doing as well as it's possible to do under the circumstances, given the ways that humans are and the sheer extent of humankind and its desires, products, and ambitions. As Kant said (Kant 1824, 388) (and Berlin 1991 [1950] echoed) "out of wood so crooked and perverse as that which man is made of, nothing absolutely straight can ever be wrought."

It would, however, be unjust to say that we "just muddle through," because we have problem-solving intentions when we, through governments and other agencies, engage with contested social, political, moral, epistemological, or ontological issues. We may, in fact, be living in "the best of all possible worlds" (Leibniz 1985, 128) (with emphasis on "possible") because, in our crooked timber, we are faced with change and limited predictability and can do no better than we do now (Blackwell and Seabrook 1993; Fairclough 1992).

Recently, there have been moves to reinvigorate the discourse of limited progress (Pinker 2011). Michael Shermer (Shermer 2015) has developed and described the meaning of the term "protopia" as follows:

> A better descriptor than utopia for what we ought to strive for is protopia— a place where progress is steadfast and measured. The visionary futurist Kevin Kelly (Kelly 2014) described it this way: "I call myself a protopian, not a utopian. I believe in progress in an incremental way where every year it's better than the year before but not by very much—just a micro amount." Instead of the 1950s imagined jump from the jalopy to the flying car, think of the decades-long cumulative improvements that led to today's smart cars with their onboard computers and navigation systems, air bags and composite metal frames and bodies, satellite radios and hands-free phones, and electric and hybrid engines. Instead of Great Leap Forward, think Small Step Upward.
>
> (Shermer 2015, 414)

Negotiation is a necessity, even for Small Steps Upward, and conflicting arguments must be considered, even when the arguments concern essentially contested concepts (Gallie 1955) that seem to resist the mutual engagement demanded by proper argument (Ehninger 1970; Walton 1996). We have to adapt continually from an unstable present into an uncertain future. We seek to assess different claims, using individual and communal values and information. Information is always imperfect and always shaped by values (Kuehberger 1995). Decisions, made by people who disagree with one another and with other systems of practice and belief, do not lead to utopia, but they have so far maintained our species. We can encourage value pluralism as a universal heuristic, but we cannot legislate to make people critical, sceptical, or reflective. There is a deep human desire for certainty and for control of our ambience and environment. Uncertainty, ambiguity, and unexpected consequences are the realities we often encounter (Tenner 1997), as Toulmin emphasizes when he recommends that "Uncertainty, disagreement, and respect for the variety of reasonable opinions replace them [aspirations towards certainty] at the centre of our preoccupations, as Montaigne always insisted that they should" (Toulmin 2009, 205). Value pluralism can help us to understand why we may feel unsettled and to define the edges of insecurity. It can help us to become "restrained partisans" (Ehninger 1970) for causes we can accept as beneficial to others as well as ourselves and our immediate groups. In this modest fashion, it opens a doorway of perception that may help us to understand and cope with our times and even to flourish amidst the vagaries of human interactions.

Notes

1. Although Quakerism has fragmented into a number of different forms of belief and practice, Quakers still identify themselves by the generic name of Friends, rather than differentiating between Liberal, Gurneyite, non-theistic, or other groupings. Liberal Quakerism espouses an ecumenical and inclusive approach to other religions and modes of thought, and its pluralism is sustained by its adherence to certain commitments to modes of behaviour, relationships to the universe, and relationships to other people. Utopian programmes, such as those of Robert Owen or William Lane, have ultimately failed because of individual cussedness, self-interest, and individual difference, because they have lacked the flexibility to cope with the pluralism that emerges when people are faced with the practical difficulties of adaptation to change and to other social demands (see, e.g. Holloway 1966).
2. Radical reflective equilibrium is a mode of ethical engagement that requires that any moral quandary should be examined using established ethical frameworks (such as principlism, virtue ethics, deontology), intuitive responses to the context, and the personal experiences of the ethicist (see DePaul 1993 [2001]).
3. Critical realism takes the view that there are external realities, but the truth about them is never fully known. "Good" processes of inquiry and reasoning may bring us closer to "truth," but processes of change move our understanding from one apparently stable point to another. Quantum mechanics provides an example of the way in which changing powers of measurement change understanding of truth (see Bhaskar 1998).

4. Foundherentism represents an attempt to reconcile the conflict between foundationalism and coherentism. Susan Haack has suggested that we necessarily seek foundations for knowledge and belief and that we must make the consequences of committing to such foundations cohere into a more or less consistent set of beliefs (see Haack 1993).
5. Appreciative inquiry aims to interrogate a disputed topic in order to define the issues under dispute. It demands both objectivity and empathic entry into the mainstream of the dispute. It aims to clarify what may be agreed between conflicting arguments as well as the nature and contents of disagreements. Generative editing describes the process whereby someone, such as a bioethicist or journal editor, examines conflicting submissions, and tries to crystalize emergent issues in such a way as to inform stakeholders in the dispute of possible insights and ways to reframe and progress the contested discourses (for appreciative inquiry, see Bushe 2013; for generative editing, see Gabler, Bornstein, and Pierce 1995).
6. To illustrate the differences, consider the following statements. Justice is a *principle* of good governance. In Western countries, the argumentative court system is *axiomatically* the right way to insure justice. The *maxim* that "Justice is blind" reflects the desirability of impartiality in the administration of justice. Principles, being broad in scope, are able to attract wider agreement. Axioms are more specific in their reference, and maxims reflect local norms and beliefs and are likely to cause more dispute between protagonists of different cultures, beliefs, and traditions.
7. Essentially contested concepts are those that develop when opposing parties recognize a problem by name but disagree on its reference and significance. Poverty provides an example. Parties of the right and left may recognize the entity of poverty and even agree on a definition. At one extreme, the left may argue that poverty is a misfortune forced onto some people, who must benefit from government assistance and support. On the right, poverty may be construed as a self-inflicted woe, expressing an inability among the poor to make their own ways in a modern world. In a neoliberal society, the emphasis on individual choice and responsibility influences attitudes towards social welfare and government intervention (see Gallie 1955).

References

Archer, M., R. Bhaskar, A. Collier, T. Lawson, and A. Norrie, eds. 1998. *Critical realism: Essential readings*. Abingdon, Oxon: Routledge.

Aristotle. 1976. *The ethics of Aristotle: The Nichomachean ethics*. Translated by J.A.K. Thomson. London: Penguin Books Ltd.

Audi, R. 2004. *The good in the right: A theory of intuition and intrinsic value*. Princeton, NJ: Princeton University Press.

Beauchamp, T.L., and J.F. Childress. 2001. *Principles of biomedical ethics*. Oxford: Oxford University Press.

Berlin, I. 1969 [1958]. Two concepts of liberty. In *Four essays on liberty*, 162–166. Oxford: Oxford University Press.

———. 1991 [1950]. *The crooked timber of humanity: Chapters in the history of ideas*. London: Fontana Press.

Bhaskar, R. 1998. Critical realism and dialectic. In *Critical realism: Essential readings*, edited by M. Archer, R. Bhaskar, A. Collier, T. Lawson, and A. Norrie, 599–605. Abingdon, Oxon: Routledge.

Blackburn, S. 2014. Human nature and science: A cautionary essay. *Behaviour* 151(2–3): 229–244.

Blackwell, T., and J. Seabrook. 1993. *The revolt against change: Towards a conserving radicalism.* London: Vintage Books.

Blendon, R.J., J.M. Benson, and J.O. Hero. 2014. Public trust in physicians: U.S. medicine in international perspective. *New England Journal of Medicine* 371(17): 1570–1572.

Bond, M.H., K. Leung, A. Au, et al. 2004. Culture-level dimensions of social axioms and their correlates across 41 cultures. *Journal of Cross-Cultural Psychology* 35(5): 548–570.

Breen, K.J., V.D. Plueckhahn, and S.M. Cordner. 1997. *Ethics, law and medical practice.* Sydney: Allen & Unwin.

Bushe, G.R. 2013. Generative process, generative outcome: The transformational potential of appreciative inquiry. In *Organizational generativity: The appreciative inquiry summit and a scholarship of transformation* (Advances in Appreciative Inquiry, Vol. 4), edited by D.L. Cooperrider, D.P. Zandee, L.N. Godwin, M. Avital, and B. Boland, 89–113. Bingley: Emerald Group Publishing Limit.

Carter, S.M., and M. Little. 2008. Justifying knowledge, justifying method, taking action: Epistemologies, methodologies and methods in qualitative research. *Qualitative Health Research* 17(10): 1316–1328.

Cheung, M.W.L., K. Leung, and K. Au. 2006. Evaluating multilevel models in cross-cultural research: An illustration with social axioms. *Journal of Cross Cultural Psychology* 37(5): 522–541.

Christman, J. 2004. Relational autonomy, liberal individualism, and the social constitution of selves. *Philosophical Studies* 117(1–2): 143–164.

Daniels, N. 1980. Reflective equilibrium and Archimedian points. *Canadian Journal of Philosophy* 10(1): 83–103.

———. 1996. *Justice and justification: Reflective equilibrium in theory and practice.* Cambridge: Cambridge University Press.

———. 2000. Accountability for reasonableness: Establishing a fair process for priority setting is easier than agreeing on principles. *British Medical Journal* 321(7272): 1300.

Daniels, N., and J.E. Sabin. 2008. Accountability for reasonableness: An update. *British Medical Journal* 337: a1850.

DePaul, M.R. 1993 [2001]. *Balance and refinement: Beyond coherence methods of moral inquiry.* London: Routledge.

Dewey, J. 1941. Propositions, warranted assertibility, and truth. *The Journal of Philosophy* 38(7): 169–186.

Ehninger, D. 1970. Argument as method: Its nature, its limitations and its uses. *Communications Monographs* 37(2): 101–110.

Engelhardt, H.T. 2011. Confronting moral pluralism in posttraditional western societies: Bioethics critically reassessed. *Journal of Medicine and Philosophy* 36(3): 243–260.

Fairclough, N. 1992. *Discourse and social change.* Cambridge: Polity Press.

Feyerabend, P. 1993. *Against method*, 3rd ed. London: Verson.

Fisher, R.J. 2016. Generic principles for resolving intergroup conflict. In *Ronald J. Fisher: A North American pioneer in interactive conflict resolution*, 87–104. Cham: Springer International Publishing.

Gabler, H.W., G. Bornstein, and G. Borland Pierce. 1995. *Contemporary German editorial theory.* Ann Arbor, MI: University of Michigan Press.

Gallie, W.B. 1955. Essentially contested concepts. *Proceedings of the Aristotelian Society* 56: 167–198.

Galston, W.A. 1999. Value pluralism and liberal political theory. *The American Political Science Review* 93(4): 769–778.

———. 2002. *Liberal pluralism: The implications of value pluralism for political theory and practice*. Cambridge: Cambridge University Press.

Gee, J.P. 1990. *Social linguistics and literacies: Ideology and discourses*. London: Falmer Press.

Geertz, C. 1964. Ideology as a cultural system. In *Ideology and its discontents*, edited by D.E. Apter, 47–76. Glencoe, IL: Free Press of Glencoe.

Gray, J. 1978. On liberty, liberalism and essential contestability. *British Journal of Political Science* 8(4): 385–402.

———. 2016. *Straw dogs: Thoughts on humans and other animals*. New York, NY: Farrar, Straus and Giroux.

Grice, H.P. 1975. Logic and conversation. In *Syntax and semantics III: Speech acts*, edited by P. Cole and J.L. Morgado, 41–58. New York, NY: Academic Press.

Haack, S. 1993. *Evidence and inquiry*. Oxford: Blackwell Publishers.

Habermas, J. 1991. Discourse ethics: Notes on a program of philosophical justification. In *The communicative ethics controversy*, edited by S. Benhabib and F. Dallmayr. Cambridge, MA: MIT Press.

———. 1992. *Moral consciousness and communicative action*. Translated by C. Lenhardt and S.W. Nicholsen. Cambridge: Polity Press.

Hart, H.L.A. 1977. Positivism and the separation of law and morals. In *The philosophy of law*, edited by R.M. Dworkin, 17–37. Oxford: Oxford University Press.

Hogan, J.C., and M.D. Schwartz. 1984. A translation of Bacon's maxims of the common law. *Law Library Journal* 77: 707–718.

Holloway, M. 1966. *Heavens on earth: Utopian communities in America, 1680–1880*. Mineola, NY: Courier Corporation.

Hui, V.K.Y., M.H. Bond, and T.S. Ng. 2006. General beliefs about the world as defensive mechanisms against death anxiety. *Omega (Westport)* 54(3): 199–214.

Hulme, M. 2009. *Why we disagree about climate change: Understanding controversy, inaction, and opportunity*. New York, NY: Cambridge University Press.

Hume, D. 1991. *An enquiry concerning human understanding*. Edited by L.A. Selby-Bigge. Oxford: Clarendon Press.

Joshanloo, M., S. Afshari, and P. Rastegar. 2010. Linking social axioms with indicators of positive interpersonal, social and environmental functioning in Iran: An exploratory study. *International Journal of Psychology* 45(4): 303–310.

Kant, I. 1824. Idea of a universal history on a cosmo-political plan. *London Magazine* 385–393.

Kantrowitz, A. 1977. The science court experiment. *Jurimetrics Journal* 17(4): 332–341.

Kelly, K. 2014. The technium. A conversation with Kevin Kelly by John Brockman. *Edge*, March 2. www.edge.org/conversation/kevin_kelly-the-technium. Accessed April 08, 2018.

Kennedy, D. 2013. The international human rights regime: Still part of the problem? In *Examining critical perspectives on human rights*, edited by R. Dickinson, E. Katselli, C. Murray and O.W. Pedersen. Cambridge: Cambridge University Press.

Kerridge, I., M. Lowe, and J. McPhee. 2005. *Ethics and the law for the health professions*. Sydney: The Federation Press.

Kuehberger, A. 1995. The framing of decisions: A new look at old problems. *Organizational Behavior & Human Decision Processes* 62(2): 230–240.

Kurman, J., and C. Ronen-Eilon. 2004. Lack of knowledge of a culture's social axioms and adaptation difficulties among immigrants. *Journal of Cross Cultural Psychology* 35(2): 192–208.

Kymlicka, W. 1989. *Liberalism, community and culture*. Oxford: Clarendon Press.

Lai, J., M. Bond, and N. Hui. 2007. The role of social axioms in predicting life satisfaction: A longitudinal study. *Journal of Happiness Studies* 8(4): 517–535.

Leibniz, G.W. 1985. *Theodicy*. Translated by E.M. Huggard. Edited by A. Farrar. Chicago, IL: Open Court.

Leung, K., M.H. Bond, S.R. DeCarrasquel, et al. 2002. Social axioms: The search for universal dimensions of general beliefs about how the world functions. *Journal of Cross-Cultural Psychology* 33(3): 286–302.

Little, M., C.F. Jordens, C. McGrath, K. Montgomery, I. Kerridge, and S.M. Carter. 2007. Pragmatic pluralism: Mutual tolerance of contested understandings between orthodox and alternative practitioners in autologous stem cell transplantation. *Social Science & Medicine* 64: 1512–1523.

Little, M., W. Lipworth, J. Gordon, P. Markham, and I. Kerridge. 2012. Values-based medicine and modest foundationalism. *Journal of Evaluation in Clinical Practice* 18(5): 1020–1026.

Loughlin, M., ed. 2014. *Debates in values-based medicine*. Cambridge: Cambridge University Press.

Low, A. 1997. The return of dialectic to its place in intellectual life. *Rhetoric Review* 15(2): 365–381.

MacKenzie, C., and N. Stoljar. 2000. *Relational autonomy: Feminist perspectives on autonomy, agency, and the social self*. Oxford: Oxford University Press.

Mandell, M., R. Keast, and D. Chamberlain. 2017. Collaborative networks and the need for a new management language. *Public Management Review* 19(3): 326–341.

Markovits, E. 2006. The trouble with being earnest: Deliberative democracy and the sincerity norm. *Journal of Political Philosophy* 14(3): 249–269.

Martin, D.K., M. Giacomini, and P.A. Singer. 2002. Fairness, accountability for reasonableness, and the views of priority setting decision-makers. *Health Policy* 61(3): 279–290.

Mazur, A. 1993. The science court: Reminiscence and retrospective. *Risk* 4: 161–170.

Mills, C. 2007. White ignorance. In *Race and epistemologies of ignorance*, edited by S. Sullivan and N. Tuana, 13–38. Albany, NY: SUNY Press.

Morgan, D.L. 2007. Paradigms lost and pragmatism regained. *Journal of Mixed Methods Research* 1(1): 48–76.

O'Neill, O. 1987. Abstraction, idealization and ideology in ethics. In *Moral philosophy and contemporary problems*, edited by J.D.G. Evans. Cambridge: Cambridge University Press.

Pinker, S. 2002. *The blank slate: The modern denial of human nature*. New York, NY: Viking Press.

———. 2011. *The better angels of our nature: The decline of violence in history and its causes*. New York, NY: Penguin Books.

Pound, R. 1921. The maxims of equity. I of maxims generally. *Harvard Law Review* 34(8): 809–836.

Prasad, V. 2015. Why Lisa Rosenbaum gets conflict of interest policies wrong. *Lown Institute Blog*, May 28. http://lowninstitute.org/news/why-lisa-rosenbaum-gets-conflict-of-interest-policies-wrong/. Accessed January 23, 2018.

Rescher, N. 1992. *Pluralism: Against the demand for consensus.* New Haven, CT: Yale University Press.

Rorty, R. 1982. *Consequences of pragmatism (Essays: 1972–1980).* Minneapolis, MN: University of Minnesota Press.

Rosenbaum, L. 2015. Beyond moral outrage: Weighing the trade-offs of COI regulation. *New England Journal of Medicine* 372(21): 2064–2068.

Shermer, M. 2015. *The moral arc, how science makes us better people.* New York, NY: Henry Holt and Company.

Steffen, W., W. Broadgate, L. Deutsch, O. Gaffney, and C. Ludwig. 2015. The trajectory of the anthropocene: The great acceleration. *The Anthropocene Review* 2(1): 81–98.

Stone, K. 2015. NEJM reignites conflict-of-interest debate with reader poll. *Health News Review,* June 2. www.healthnewsreview.org/2015/06/nejm-reignites-conflict-of-interest-debate-with-reader-poll/. Accessed March 07, 2018.

Tauber, A.I., and S. Sarkar. 1993. The ideology of the human genome project. *Journal of the Royal Society of Medicine* 86(9): 537–540.

Tenner, E. 1997. *Why things bite back: New technology and the revenge effect.* London: Fourth Estate.

Tetlock, P.E. 1986. A value pluralism model of ideological reasoning. *Journal of Personality and Social Psychology* 50(4): 819.

Thornton, P.H., and W. Ocasio. 1999. Institutional logics and the historical contingency of power in organizations: Executive succession in the higher education publishing industry, 1958–1990. *American Journal of Sociology* 105(3): 801–843.

Thornton, P.H., W. Ocasio, and M. Lounsbury. 2012. *The institutional logics perspective: A new approach to culture, structure, and process.* Oxford: Oxford University Press on Demand.

Toulmin, S.E. 1972. *Human understanding: The collective use and evolution of concepts.* Princeton, NJ: Princeton University Press.

———. 2009. *Return to reason.* Cambridge, MA: Harvard University Press.

Walton, D. 1989. Dialogue theory for critical thinking. *Argumentation* 3(2): 169–184.

———. 1996. *Argument structure: A pragmatic theory* (Toronto Studies in Philosophy). Toronto, ON: University of Toronto Press.

———. 2006. Examination dialogue: An argumentation framework for critically questioning an expert opinion. *Journal of Pragmatics* 38(5): 745–777.

Walzer, M. 1995. *Spheres of justice: A defence of pluralism and equality.* Oxford: Blackwell Publishers.

Weart, S.R. 2003. *The discovery of global warming.* Cambridge, MA: Harvard University Press.

9 Making Sense of Professional Conflicts and Quandaries

Wendy Lipworth and Kathleen Montgomery

The five empirical chapters in this volume paint a rich picture of physicians' role-related conflicts and quandaries. The two conceptual chapters that follow offer some innovative ways to think about the challenges facing medical professionals as they strive to make sense of the changing landscape within healthcare. In this concluding chapter, we first draw together the empirical observations presented herein to suggest insights and commonalities about (1) the types of role-related conflicts that can arise in medical practice, (2) the ways physicians experience these conflicts, and (3) suggestions for managing role-related conflicts that emerge from the studies. We next review the contributions of the two conceptual chapters, each offering new innovative frameworks through which to understand the variety of role-related conflicts and quandaries confronting today's medical professionals: Jordens provides a fresh lens for explaining why role-related conflicts seem so intractable and value-laden, and Little provides a thoughtful way to move forward, even in the midst of conflicts.

Types of Role-Related Conflicts

The empirical studies reported here have illuminated three broad types of role-related conflicts: (1) those in which physicians are focused on only one role—patient care, for example—but have to contend with competing norms and values in their fulfilment of the role, (2) those in which physicians' personal interests compete or conflict with their role-related obligations, and (3) those in which the obligations associated with two or more roles are in tension.

A clear illustration of the first type of role-related conflict (competing values within a given role) can be found in Chapter 2 (Jordens and Montgomery). Here, physicians strive to respect their patients' autonomy by obtaining informed consent and fulfilling patients' wishes, but this goal can conflict with physicians' determination to respect their patients' equally autonomous decision *not to be informed* as well as physicians' determination to promote interventions that are clinically necessary, safe, and effective. This type of role-related conflict is also evident in Chapter 3 (Ghinea et al.), which describes the conflict that arises when physicians want to practice medicine according to established regulatory standards while providing particular patients with whatever care is most appropriate *for them*. In so doing, they experience a tension regarding the meaning of high-quality prescribing. Similarly, in Chapter 4, Pace and colleagues have made visible the views and experiences of physicians who prescribe high-cost cancer medicines and are tasked with the conflicting need to provide patients with hope and compassionate care while making decisions that are based on evidence of safety and efficacy. In all three cases, the physicians are occupying one professional role—patient care—but there are conflicting ways of fulfilling the obligations associated with the role.

The second type of role-related conflict (self-interest versus external obligation) is illustrated in Chapter 5 (Lipworth and Montgomery), which describes the conflicts that arise when physicians interact with the pharmaceutical industry. This situation presents the potential for self-interest (e.g. monetary gain or career advancement), which may interfere with their commitment to patients, research participants, or the public good. Also, in Chapter 6, Gallagher describes the way in which physicians' concern for their own career advancement (by advocating for resources to be allocated to their health services) can lead them to make macroallocation recommendations that are not in the population's interest.

The remaining examples in the volume illustrate the third type of role-related conflict, where the obligations associated with two roles are in tension. For example, in Chapter 5, Lipworth and Montgomery describe the experiences of clinicians who work for the pharmaceutical industry and have to balance their obligations as healthcare professionals against their obligations as employees of industry. We also see this scenario in Chapter 4 (Pace et al.) and Chapter 6 (Gallagher), who describe the tensions experienced by clinicians who need to advocate for their patients while advocating for the sustainability and efficiency of the health system in which they are embedded. Gallagher refers to this type of role-related conflict as "dual agency" in order to distinguish it from the "conflict of interest" that arises when physicians' self-interest conflicts with their population-level obligations.

It is clear from these examples that not only may medical professionals encounter more than one broad type of role-related conflict but also that a single situation—such as prescribing high-cost medicines (Chapter 4) or fulfilling formal macroallocation roles (Chapter 6)—can simultaneously create more than one type of role-related conflict.

How Physicians Experience Role-Related Conflicts

In addition to describing *types* of role-related conflicts, the chapters in this volume also reveal the ways that these conflicts are *experienced* by physicians. It is noteworthy that there is considerable variation among the studies with respect to the degree of cognitive dissonance reported by physicians; in some cases, the dissonance is considerable—that is conflicts are also experienced as quandaries—whereas in other cases, physicians seem able to navigate role-related tensions with little evidence of concern.

Jordens and Montgomery (Chapter 2) describe their participants as experiencing considerable "dismay" when patients refuse to engage fully with educational activities, followed by "uneasiness" if patients subsequently complain that they would have made different decisions if they had been adequately forewarned. The authors also observe considerable anger on the part of health professionals—manifested in a tendency to shift the blame onto patients for failing to make use of educational opportunities. Similarly, when patients insist on clinical courses of action that physicians cannot condone, "the situation is framed as an ethical quandary, and the patient's autonomy is placed under the hermeneutics of suspicion" (this volume, 21). Jordens and Montgomery summarize their findings by noting sources of frustration that stem from falling short of the goal of informing patients, the incompleteness of the consent genre, and the paradox that arises when patients exercise their autonomy by refusing to become informed.

In contrast, the physicians in Ghinea et al.'s study (Chapter 3) do not express much "confusion or paralysis" about off-label prescribing, despite the ambiguous status of the practice. The interviews do reveal some discomfort with "experimenting" on patients where evidence is unclear and the practice is unsupported by the profession, yet even here, the discomfort has "little to do with the regulatory status of the product itself, but rather the capabilities of the practicing physician" (this volume, 32). Participants recognize that uncertainty is inevitable in clinical practice, and they question the social authority of research and regulatory processes. The authors of Chapter 4 (Pace et al.) are not definitive about whether their participants experience discomfort from role-related conflicts or quandaries. Rather, they focus on avoidance strategies as a means to both prevent and manage cognitive dissonance.

Additional ways that medical professionals experience role-related conflicts are illustrated in Chapter 5 (Lipworth and Montgomery) in their examination of professionals' interactions with the pharmaceutical industry. First, in their analysis of the Rosenbaum debate, the authors describe two opposing groups—one that is highly critical of industry interactions and one that is supportive of such interactions. Professionals in both camps are certain of their views, such that there is little internal cognitive dissonance on either side; both are correspondingly certain about how industry interactions should be regulated. Next, in their study of medical professionals who are employed by pharmaceutical companies, the authors find a group of people who are comfortable with their dual roles—a position that is made possible by the belief that industry goals and public health goals are largely compatible and by their acceptance of multiple levels of regulation as supportive of their actions and decisions.

Gallagher (Chapter 6) explicitly sets out to explore if and how participating doctors appreciated role-related conflicts as an ethical issue and concludes that while both conflict of interest and dual agency are features of the mac-roallocation process "[doctors] (do) not . . . view these phenomena as ethi-cally troubling at a personal level and construct . . . them not as challenges to medical professional ethics but as part of the social process of priority setting" (this volume, 98–99). With respect to personal conflict of interest, Gallagher's participants "den(y) being influenced by either the desire for personal financial gain, or the desire to progress their careers" (this volume, 93). With respect to dual agency, doctors avoid cognitive dissonance by compartmentalizing their dual roles. To the extent that doctors are ethi-cally troubled, this is primarily focused on "the ethical ramifications of pro-cedural deficiencies, such as bureaucratic inefficiency and behaviours and structures that disadvantage certain types of participants" (this volume, 93).

Managing Role-Related Conflicts: Suggestions From the Studies

The authors of the empirical chapters offer several views about how role-related conflicts might be managed. These ideas range from the modest to the aspirational and include interventions targeted at modifying individual attitudes, shifts in professional codes of ethics, and regulatory changes at the system level.

For example, Jordens and Montgomery (Chapter 2) emphasize the limited capacity that physicians have to practice medicine according to the ideals of the day, arguing that patient autonomy endures the rigours of illness and onerous treatments in a partial, distorted and sometimes disruptive ways and that shared decision-making exists within limits that are "the points at which the parties to clinical decisions can exercise their autonomy by making *unilateral* decisions" (this volume, 24). Their suggestions for manag-ing role-related conflicts are correspondingly modest, focused on *individual attitudes* of clinicians, who need to accept (and even embrace) the fact that "aspirational models of care need to be simplified, routinized, and standard-ized" (this volume, 24) and that "there will always be a need for judgement when professionals are faced with difficult and/or exceptional cases" (this volume, 24). They also caution against "absolutism in theory" and "over-zealousness in practice" that seek to implement and enforce ideal models of care in ways that "overreach practical limits" (this volume, 24).

Ghinea et al. (Chapter 3) accept their participants' view that the ability to justify a clinical decision—rather than its regulatory status—should be the key factor separating a legitimate decision from an illegitimate one. The authors call for change in the way *system-level regulation* is understood and used, arguing that "the purpose of regulatory approval should primarily be to establish initial clinical parameters for newly introduced medicines, not necessarily to provide any specific guidance around acceptable uses" (this volume, 39). In this way, the authors suggest that the ambiguities sur-rounding off-label prescribing can be dealt with not by changing physicians' attitudes or clinical practice but rather by changing the system from which the ambiguous concept arises. Ghinea et al. also call for a shift in thinking within medicine as a whole, perhaps through changes to *professional codes of ethics*, from one that demands adherence to the tenets of evidence-based medicine (narrowly construed) to one that recognizes the value of "reasonableness" in judgement and decision-making.

Pace et al. (Chapter 4) focus their discussion on ways of preventing or managing physicians' cognitive dissonance. These authors argue that it might be possible to do so by reassuring physicians that the interests of the broader healthcare system can still be served if they privilege the interests of their individual patients. This can be accomplished, the authors propose, by a deeper understanding of the macro systems of health technology assessment and resource allocation. In so doing, physicians might gain more confidence in deferring to restrictions placed by administrators as well as become more aware of alternative access pathways. The authors note that dissonance might nevertheless persist but could be better tolerated by "reassuring doctors that there are a number of possible correct actions when we have greater healthcare needs than resources can support" (this volume, 63) and by reminding physicians that "we live in a liberal democratic society, where individuals hold diverse views which may all be equally valid" (this volume, 63). While most of their suggestions focus on *reassuring and educating doctors*, they also note the importance of *system-level change* in the form of "strengthening resource allocation processes so that it is easier for physicians to focus on advocating for the interests of their patients without fear of undermining these processes to the public detriment" (this volume, 63).

Lipworth and Montgomery (Chapter 5) also note the connection between *individual attitudes* and *system-level regulations*. They suggest that regulation of role-related conflict need not be thought of as a win–lose situation; rather, they propose that a greater appreciation of different levels of regulation can be valuable and that—somewhat paradoxically—medicine might be able to learn something from industry about how to think about and manage such conflicts in a multi-layered and non-punitive way.

Finally, Gallagher (Chapter 6) argues that doctors conceptualize the problems of dual agency and conflict of interest as existing in the social, rather than internal, world. Thus, Gallagher argues against conflict-management approaches that are "physician focused—prescribing attitudes and actions for doctors to take" because this "overestimates both doctors' insight into potential conflicts and the degree to which they are troubled by them" and "overlooks the social context of macro-allocation," which is "a deliberative process that brings together a plurality of voices and skills to argue the merits of a range of claims and norms" (this volume, 91). While Gallagher sees value in ethical education for individual doctors, she argues that the focus should be less on "resolution of physician ethical unease" and more on *professional codes* that "promote sensitivity to context," alert doctors to "pluralistic policy development models and their participants," and emphasize "humility and collegiality" (this volume, 100).

Drawing on Innovative Conceptual Frameworks

The two closing chapters by Jordens and by Little offer new conceptual ways to understand, first, why the sorts of conflicts presented in this volume often do result in quandaries for which there may be no obvious resolution and, second, ways of moving forward in an environment of moral ambiguity and value pluralism.

In Chapter 7, Jordens returns to foundational sociological questions of professional power, which implicitly shape the roles and responsibilities of clinicians and underlie role-related conflicts. He traces how different understandings of professional power have been used to explain—and critique—both medicine's expansion into new jurisdictions of health and its "reduction" to the molecular level. He illustrates how new "ideologies of care," including those that espouse humanistic values (e.g. "patient-centred care") can be challenging for clinicians when they "seek to override the need for ethical judgement" or "disrupt and compete with ways of 'doing' care that have congealed into normal accepted practice" (this volume, 122). Jordens argues that paradigm shifts in the theory and practice of care can function as positive signs of a medical profession responsive to criticism while also serving as a source of conflict, such as those reflected in the studies reported in this volume.

In Chapter 8, Little joins Jordens in recognizing the inevitability of change and the challenges such change can generate for clinicians caught in the midst of dealing with differing stakeholders who have interests in their multiple roles. Little observes:

> Money and power and status and vulnerability together make a confusing moral and practical mélange. Doctors and their colleagues must somehow make sense of the resulting complexity, making their way through murky paths of uncertainty and risk.
>
> (this volume, 125)

Using illustrations from the empirical chapters in the book, Little explains that it is essential to examine the values that underpin the phenomena of disagreement and quandary. He then draws on the concept of value pluralism as a heuristic to guide engagement during situations when medical professionals are faced with countervailing tensions such as those reported here. The goal of such engagement is to appreciate and balance multiple norms, beliefs, and practices without imposing a new set of norms. He notes that while "there is a deep human desire for certainty and for control of our ambience and environment. Uncertainty, ambiguity, and unexpected consequences are the realities we often encounter" (this volume, 139). At the same time, he concludes that value-pluralist approach can open "a doorway of perception that may help us to understand and cope with our times and even to flourish amidst the vagaries of human interactions" (this volume, 139).

Contributor Biographies

Siun Gallagher is a final-year PhD candidate at The University of Sydney, Faculty of Medicine and Health, Sydney Health Ethics, exploring the ethical issues involved in doctors' participation as technical experts in healthcare priority setting. Her areas of interest include physician advocacy, the ethics of healthcare resource allocation, and justice in policymaking. Her work has been published in *Health Care Analysis*, *NSW Public Health Journal*, and *Heart, Lung and Circulation*. She has degrees in medicine from Trinity College, Dublin and in public health from The University of Sydney. Prior to commencing her current research, she occupied a range of senior management positions in the public health system in New South Wales, principally in the areas of policy, planning, and clinical service development.

Narcyz Ghinea is a postdoctoral researcher at The University of Sydney, Faculty of Medicine and Health, Sydney Health Ethics. His research focuses on the interplay between evidence, ethics, economics, and decision-making in health technology assessment of medicines. He is particularly interested in the tension between autonomy and solidarity in the development of health policy. In his work, he draws on his diverse professional experiences as a mathematician developing decision models for surgeons, as a policy officer at peak government agencies working on medication and patient safety, and as a health manager with responsibility for implementing projects in the public hospital system.

Christopher Jordens is Associate Professor in Bioethics at The University of Sydney, Faculty of Medicine and Health, Sydney Health Ethics. For the last twenty years, he has worked closely with colleagues and students in the health professions and in various academic disciplines. He helped to establish Sydney Health Ethics (formerly the Centre for Values, Ethics and the Law in Medicine), where he is currently a Deputy Director. He was a founding editor of the *Journal of Bioethical Inquiry* and played a leading role in creating the Sydney postgraduate bioethics programme, in which he has taught philosophy and sociology of medicine since 2006. He has published in a wide variety of academic journals and has been a chief investigator on research projects related to cancer medicine, health journalism and advertising, and bioethics. He recently held an appointment as coordinator of postgraduate research in the School of Public Health.

Ian Kerridge is an internationally recognized scholar in bioethics and the philosophy of medicine. From 2003 to 2015, he served as Director of Sydney Health Ethics (formerly the Centre for Values, Ethics, and the Law in Medicine). He is currently Professor of Bioethics and Medicine at The University of Sydney, Faculty of Medicine and Health, Sydney Health Ethics and Haematologist/Bone Marrow Transplant Physician at Royal North Shore Hospital, Sydney. His research focuses on the philosophical, moral, and sociocultural concepts, frameworks, and issues that underpin health, health policy, and biomedicine including in public health, research, and clinical care. He has secured over $28 million in competitive research grants and has over three hundred peer-reviewed publications on ethics, medical philosophy, and haematology.

Wendy Lipworth is a bioethicist and health social scientist and Associate Professor at The University of Sydney, Faculty of Medicine and Health, Sydney Health Ethics. Her research focuses on the ethics and politics of pharmaceutical innovation, with a particular focus on therapeutics research using databanks, big data, and real-world evidence; access to "unproven" therapeutic interventions; and industry influence and conflict of interest. She has been supported by National Health and Medical Research Council (NHMRC) scholarships and fellowships throughout her career and is currently supported by a NHMRC Career Development Fellowship. She has been a lead chief investigator on two NHMRC project grants focused on access to high-cost cancer medicines and conflicts of interest in health and medicine and has published extensively in international journals and books. Her work integrates sociological and philosophical theories with information about stakeholders' values to promote policies and practices that are attuned to social and political complexity.

Miles Little is Emeritus Professor of Surgery at The University of Sydney and Founding Director of the Centre for Values, Ethics, and the Law in Medicine (now Sydney Health Ethics). During his medical career, he served as Foundation Professor of Surgery at Westmead Hospital and was Co-founder and Foundation President of the World Association of Hepatic, Pancreatic and Biliary Surgeons. In 2014, he was made an Officer of the Order of Australia (AO) "for distinguished service to medicine through the development and promotion of public policy on medical values, ethics and law." In keeping with the theme of this book, he advocates a rebalancing of science and humanism in healthcare, along with an acceptance of complexity and uncertainty. His method of analysis has been described as grounded in the sense of being tied to contingencies of experience, place, history, and culture. He has published over three hundred journal articles in medicine, social science, philosophy, and ethics, a collection of poetry, and books on surgery, patient experience, and philosophy.

Kathleen Montgomery is Professor of the Graduate Division and Emerita Professor of Organizations and Management at the University of California, Riverside. For many years, she also has held the title of Honorary Associate at The University of Sydney, Faculty of Medicine and Health, Sydney Health Ethics. She is a Fellow of the Academy of Social Sciences and was awarded the University of California Edward A. Dickson Emerita Professorship in 2014. She has served as an elected officer, including Chair, of the Health Care Management Division of the Academy of Management. Her PhD in sociology is from New York University, where she began her research on the medical profession and relationships between professionals and their environment.

Bronwen Morrell is a PhD candidate and research academic at The University of Sydney, Faculty of Medicine and Health, Sydney Health Ethics and Editor-in-Chief (Production) at the *Journal of Bioethical Inquiry*. Since 2005, she has worked as a researcher, exploring wide-ranging issues including public trust in the context of tumour tissue banking, certainty and uncertainty in patient experiences of advanced ovarian cancer, power and control in health journalists' relationships with industry, and intersectionality in the discourse surrounding animal use in traditional and complementary medicines. Her work has been published in *Social Science and Medicine*, *Nature*, *The Medical Journal of Australia*, *Qualitative Health Research*, *The American Journal of Bioethics*, and elsewhere.

Jessica Pace is a PhD candidate at The University of Sydney, Faculty of Medicine and Health, Sydney Health Ethics, with undergraduate degrees in biochemistry, law, and pharmacy. She is pursuing research that examines stakeholder values and beliefs surrounding accelerated access to medicines, including initiatives that bypass or circumvent existing regulatory processes in order to provide faster and/or broader access to new therapies. She has published in this area and has received academic prizes and scholarships for both her undergraduate and postgraduate studies.

Miriam Wiersma trained in psychology and has worked as a family counsellor and community development officer for several not-for-profit organizations. She completed her Master of Public Health at The University of Sydney and is a research assistant at The University of Sydney, Faculty of Medicine and Health, Sydney Health Ethics. She is currently doing a Master of Philosophy at Sydney Health Ethics with her project entitled "The Allure of Biomedical Innovation: What Are the Social and Psychological Drivers for Doctors' use of Innovative Treatments?" Her areas of interest include power, status, and stigma processes within the medical profession, non-financial conflicts of interest in biomedical research and clinical practice, and clinical practice innovation. Her work has been published in *Journal of Medical Ethics* and *The British Medical Journal*.

Index

Page numbers in italics indicate figures and in bold indicate tables on the corresponding pages.

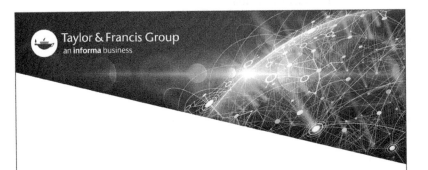

For Product Safety Concerns and Information please contact our EU
representative GPSR@taylorandfrancis.com Taylor & Francis Verlag GmbH,
Kaufingerstraße 24, 80331 München, Germany

Printed and bound by CPI Group (UK) Ltd, Croydon, CR0 4YY
01/05/2025
01858414-0003